Harry Truman and
The Human Family

Harry Truman and The Human Family

Frank K. Kelly

CAPRA PRESS
SANTA BARBARA

Cover design and book design by Frank Goad, Santa Barbara
Cover photograph courtesy of Harry S. Truman Library

LIBRARY OF CONGRESS CATALOGUING-IN-PUBLICATION DATA

Kelly, Frank K., 1914-
Harry Truman and the human family / Frank K. Kelly.
p.   cm.
ISBN 0-88496-432-9 (alk. paper)
1. Truman, Harry S., 1884-1972. 2. Presidents—United States—Election
—1948. 3. Kelly, Frank K., 1914- . 4. Campaign speeches—United States
—History—20th century.   I. Title.
E815.K45 1998
324.973'0918—dc21
98-8787
CIP

Capra Press
Post Office 2068
Santa Barbara, CA 93120

DEDICATION

TO ALL THE INSPIRING PEOPLE who have guided me, chided me, taught me, delighted me, encouraged me, amazed me, shocked me, thrilled me, debated me, challenged me, aroused me, forgiven me, shaken me, startled me, and shaped me as I have leaped from place to place, from world to world, in a long and wonderful life:

My Celtic ancestors, whose joys and sorrows are in my blood;

My grandparents and my parents, who struggled with my wild nature;

My radiant wife, Barbara, a poet, musician, and mystic;

My sons and grandsons, gifted and handsome;

My daughters-in-law, brilliant and beautiful;

All my friends in many enterprises;

All the people who voted for Harry Truman.

With special appreciation for the men with whom I worked in the Truman campaign of 1948, supplying materials for many of the speeches he gave: Bill Batt; Kenneth Birkhead; Johannes Hoeber; Philip Dreyer; John Barriere; and David Lloyd.

And deep gratitude to Christine Boesch, who read the manuscript and gave me valuable suggestions for the whole book.

"Only by helping the least fortunate of its members to help themselves can the human family achieve the decent, satisfying life that is the right of all people ...."

—HARRY S. TRUMAN, in his inaugural addres as
President of the United States, January 20, 1949

CONTENTS

CONTENTS

FOREWORD

WHEN I WAS A YOUNG MAN I plunged reluctantly into a political battle—a struggle for the survival of a besieged President who had been deserted by many of his former allies, who was regarded by many Washington observers as a misfit and a failure, who had a Missouri accent and a choppy speaking style, who was supposed to be unable to arouse the voters he needed to win an election in 1948.

I had the unexpected joy of working for a dauntless man who made me understand the responsibilities of citizens, a genial leader with a zest for public service, a man with tremendous energy and an enormous capacity for work, who believed in the power of "facts" and the value of "plain words." He made hundreds of speeches from the back end of a train that year—reaching 12 million people. He did more than speak—he listened to the voices of those millions who came out to hear him. He welcomed their questions. He wanted every voice to be heard.

Many volumes have been written about Truman's battles, his far-reaching proposals, his triumphs and trials. This book focuses on my own participation in the "whistle stop" speeches he used to reach the people in 1948, and my efforts as one of a group of young men who fought for Truman's program in the Senate in the tumultuous years between 1949 and 1952. We were often frustrated and we felt that we often failed—but we were proud to serve under Harry Truman's banner.

The Truman we knew—the man depicted in the following pages—was a warm-hearted gentle person who cared about every human being on earth, every member of the human family. He spoke with me—and others—freely about the painful decisions he had to make. He took on the burdens of the world—and responded lovingly to my mother when she chided him in the Oval Office about "mistakes" she thought he had made.

Truman is brilliantly alive in my memory and in the recollections of all who knew him. His message of hope for humanity is worth heeding at all times. He will live among us as long as democracy survives.

—FRANK K. KELLY

PART ONE

WORKING UNDER TRUMAN'S BANNER

CHAPTER ONE

A WAKE-UP CALL FROM THE WHITE HOUSE

To celebrate the completion of a book, I went to McSorley's Old Ale House in New York one night in April, 1948. I had too much of that smooth drink and I fell into a heavy slumber when I returned to my apartment in Patchin Place. I overslept—and missed the train I had planned to take to Vermont, where my wife and son were staying with friends. That long sleep changed my life forever.

The ringing of the telephone close to my bed aroused me from a troubled dream. When I opened my eyes, brilliant sunlight dazzled me. I seized the receiver. "This is the White House calling," a strong feminine voice informed me. "We want to talk to Mr. Frank Kelly. Is he there?"

In my days as a reporter for the Associated Press and the Kansas City Star I had made many calls to disturb people, and I had received calls of many kinds. But the mention of the White House shook me. I didn't have any connection with the incumbent president, although I had seen him several times in Kansas City. The book I had just finished for the Atlantic Monthly Press dealt with Truman's drive to compel Joseph Stalin to remove Soviet troops from Iran or risk a war. But I didn't think anybody on Truman's staff had heard about the book.

"What kind of a gag is this?" I said, sitting up in the bed. "It is not a gag, sir," the telephone operator said sharply. "Am I speaking to Mr. Kelly?" "You are," I answered. "What do you want?" "Just a moment," she said. Then a hearty masculine voice boomed into the receiver. "Frank, this is Bill Batt. I'm calling you from Clark Clifford's office. President Truman is going to make two or three hundred speeches this year and he needs some writers. We've been told that you're a good one. A friend of yours has informed us that you've just done a book about Truman's handling of the crisis in Iran, and he thought you might be available." "How did you get into this?" I demanded. "I've heard of Clark Clifford but I've never heard of you."

"I ran for Congress on the Democratic ticket in Philadelphia and I got some help from Clifford," Batt said. "I didn't get into Congress but Clifford asked me to recruit a group of young guys to do a lot of work for Truman's campaign this year." "Two or three hundred speeches," I said. "I still think this might be a pipe dream." Batt laughed so loudly that I had to wince. He went on, "Your friend is right here with us, Kenny Birkhead. I'll put him on."

When I heard Birkhead's familiar Missouri twang, I knew I was facing a situation I had never expected to encounter—an invitation to get into a presidential campaign. Birkhead and I had been friends since the 1930s, when we had been students together at the University of Kansas City. We were both veterans of World War II and we had been active in the American Veterans Committee. I learned later Batt had been in the AVC, too and had asked Birkhead to help him in rounding up researchers and writers for Truman.

"You sound shocked," Birkhead said. "I guess you hadn't heard about my job in Washington." "That White House operator woke me up," I said. "I went to McSorley's last night with Martin Quigley. I didn't think this was real."

"It's real, man," Birkhead snapped. "The President has approved a proposal to create a Research Division at the Democratic National Committee, and five or six of us are going to be assigned there. We're going to gather ideas and materials for the speeches Truman's going to make on this trips through the country by train. We'll work on the back-platform talks and some of the big ones in the cities, too. Do you want to be in on it?"

When Franklin Roosevelt died in April 1945—and Truman had moved into the White House—I was an army correspondent with American troops in northern France. A man in my unit, who heard that I came from Kansas City, asked what course our new Commander in Chief would pursue. I was stunned. I told him I thought Truman was a good man but I had never expected him to be president. I had grown up in the age of Roosevelt and I couldn't imagine anyone else in that office.

Birkhead's question was hard for me to handle. I knew that Truman had made some tremendous decisions, but I didn't think he had provided the kind of inspiring leadership Roosevelt had displayed. I wasn't sure that Truman was deeply committed to the liberal programs Roosevelt had launched.

"Come on, Frank," he said. "Did you hear my question?" "Let me talk to Barbara and a few friends," I answered. "You know I've been critical of some of the things Truman has done. I don't want to write speeches that will endorse every action he has taken. I don't like political speeches. I've never been in politics."

"Listen, I've got principles, too," Birkhead said. "You know I'm not a political hack. We'll divide the speech assignments on a wide range of topics, and you can work on the ones you can honestly handle." I sat on the edge of my bed in New York, thinking of what I was facing. "Give me a day or two to consider it," I said. Birkhead's reply gave me a jolt. "You can't have a day. We haven't got much time. Call us back by 4 o'clock this afternoon. We've got other names on our list of writers."

I'm sure you have," I said. "I'm grateful to you for thinking of me, Kenny." "I was thinking of Truman, too," Birkhead said. "He's a great guy and he deserves all the help we can give him. I was glad to get a chance to work for him and I thought you would be, too. He's facing a hard fight and you should be in it with him. If he's kicked out of the White House, the New Deal will go down, too." The Roosevelt program called "the New Deal" had helped millions of people to recover from the depression of the 1930s—including my father and many of our friends. As a Senator, Truman had supported all of Roosevelt's measures. I admired him for that.

When my conversation with Birkhead ended, I stretched out in the bed in the Greenwich Village apartment, staring at the green tree visible through a window. There had been many surprises in my life, but this was one I didn't know how to handle. In my interplanetary teens I had been a spinner of science fiction, writing about imaginary voyages through space and time for *Amazing Stories* and other magazines. A professor at my university had persuaded me to drop such wild pursuits and I had gone into journalism—first on the *Kansas City Star* and then with the *AP* in New York. I had been awarded a Nieman Fellowship by Harvard for my achievements as a journalist. I had been a war correspondent and a contributor to many publications, ranging from *The Atlantic Monthly* to *The New Yorker*.

I had never considered the possibility of getting into politics. My years as a reporter and editor on a Republican newspaper, the *Star*, had made me skeptical of all politicians. I knew Harry Truman had accepted the support of the corrupt Pendergast machine in Kansas City. Although Truman was personally "clean," he had never repudiated his friendship with Jim and Tom Pendergast, who had aided his rise to power.

Truman was a major figure in the novel I had just finished. I had been an *AP* reporter at the United Nations in 1946, when the United States and the Soviet Union clashed over the presence of Soviet troops in Iran. I had felt the anguish of UN officials and diplomats who feared that the confrontation between the two superpowers might lead to a third World War. My book focused on the strenuous efforts of correspondents for news agencies, who were trying to discover what was going on behind the scenes. In doing research for this story (published later under the title of "An Edge of Light") I became convinced Truman had been extremely bold in his exercise of presidential power.

In any case, Truman's gamble had paid off. Unwilling to engage in a direct collision with the United States, the Soviets pulled their troops out. I recognized the fact that Truman had done what he thought was right, but I was horrified by the power of a daring president to bring the United States to the brink of war without a public debate. As he did in many instances, Truman felt he represented the people and he acted for the people. Yet, I believed that the people should be openly consulted in any emergency possibly involving a military combat in the nuclear age.

In my apartment in Patchin Place that morning, I wished I had not lost the deep faith of my Catholic boyhood. I couldn't pray to a God who had vanished from my life. Finally, I rose to my feet, took a shower, and got dressed. Then I called my wife. I had faith in her honesty and wisdom. When Barbara came to the telephone in Vermont, I wondered how many Republicans up there might be listening to our conversation. She was staying with friends who had an open line.

"If you think Truman is better than any of the other candidates, as I certainly do, you should be for him," Barbara said quickly. "You're not going to go for Henry Wallace or Strom Thurmond or Tom Dewey." "I don't have to get involved in it at all," I said.

Barbara responded after a moment of silence, "If you pass it up, you'll always feel you missed something big. I know you well enough to be sure of that; either way, there'll be some consequences." "I'll have to be in Washington for months if I get into this," I reminded her. "I think it's important for you to help Truman if you can," Barbara said. "But I'll accept the decision you make—whatever it is."

When I talked with Martin Quigley, he groaned, "Don't do it, man. Truman is no Roosevelt. He tried to handle the job, but he flopped. He's going down the tube."

Then I telephoned Charlie Morton, the Atlantic Monthly Press editor who had encouraged me to write my novel. Morton was angry at me. Morton was hot-tempered and he didn't have much use for politicians of any kind.

"It's a bad idea, Frank," Morton sputtered. "Don't get into that political swamp. Truman is a sure loser. You're a good man and a good writer. Start another book. Stick with your writing. We'll get you a job here in Boston with plenty of time to write." "What kind of a job?" I asked. "They are expanding the department of journalism at Boston University," Morton said. "I know Jack Gleason, a guy over there. You're a Nieman Fellow and your book's going to make a splash. They'll be happy to have you there." "Thanks, Charlie," I said. "I never had any courses in journalism myself." "That doesn't matter," Morton grunted. "You've got a track record."

Teaching at Boston University would be an interesting experiment, but I didn't want to move to Boston and I knew that Barbara didn't want to go back there. We had enjoyed our time in Cambridge and Boston when I had been a Nieman Fellow at Harvard, but we liked the swift pace of life in New York better. Yet we had less than five hundred dollars in our bank account, and we had a child to feed. Even if my book sold well, it would be quite a while before money rolled in.

"Thanks, Charlie," I said. "You're the kind of friend I'll always appreciate. You've been wonderful to me. I'll let you know when I've decided what to do." "You've got a chance now to get launched as a writer," Morton responded. "If you go to Washington you'll waste it. Truman can get a lot of guys to write speeches for him. You don't need to do it." Morton hung up. I went to see my literary agent, Mary Abbott, the senior partner in the McIntosh & Otis agency. She had given me valuable advice when I had been struggling to finish my novel. She was a bright and witty woman.

"I can't see why you're hesitating," she said at once. "How many times will you have a chance to get into a presidential campaign at the top level? You might get a splendid book out of it, whether Truman wins or loses. It will be an experience that will change your life. Not many writers ever have such a chance."

"Do you personally think Truman has been a good president?" I asked her. "Do you think he deserves to be in there for four more years?" "I think he has been a better president that we deserve," Mrs. Abbott responded. "I'm sure you can help him if you decide to get into it, but you won't swing the election. You won't have to carry it on your shoulders. It will really be up to Truman and the voters."

The idea that Truman had been a better president than we had deserved immediately shocked me. I had taken it for granted that presidents had to live up to the highest expectations of the people. If the people weren't engaging in the processes of self-government, they weren't measuring up to the demands of democracy. Truman had certainly been struggling with the problems of establishing justice and peace in the world, while many citizens simply sniped at him or stayed on the sidelines.

Mrs. Abbott wasn't a political expert but she was a thoughtful person who had read many volumes of history. When I had been producing my book on the showdown between Truman and Stalin over Iran, she had noted that Truman had handled that crisis very carefully. Some observers had called Truman a president "who shot from the hip" but Truman hadn't done that on many occasions. She believed he had revealed the qualities of a good leader in a dangerous and difficult age.

"What if Truman loses this year, as he probably will?" I said. "Won't it affect the rest of my life?" "Of course, it would," she answered. "It would affect all of our lives, but you're a writer. Everything is grist for a writer's mind. If Truman loses, the pain of going through a hard battle and suffering a defeat would make you understand what a leader in these times has to endure. If he wins, that will change you, too. You'll probably be offered a lasting job in Washington and you'll probably take it. But you can use everything you do and everything that happens to you. You must know that." "Yes," I said. "And now I certainly know how you'll vote in November." She nodded. "For Truman. I think he'll win, whether you work for him or not. He's a real man. He stands on his own feet. He accepts responsibility for what he does. He'll talk to everybody he can reach and he'll listen to people, too. He'll wake the voters up, just as the White House woke you up this morning. Those things will count for him in the end."

I thanked Mrs. Abbott for her advice and went to see Quigley, who had a spacious office in a building a few blocks away. When I told him my wife and my literary agent had convinced me I should join Truman's campaign staff, he was concerned about my mental stability. If Truman was crushed in an electoral landslide—as the polls indicated—I would be regarded as a man with bad judgment. My intelligence would be questioned. "That's a possibility," I said. "But I've taken other chances. When I left the *Star* in Kansas City, I didn't know whether I could survive in New York. I sold pieces to magazines. I got by."

"Hal Boyle helped you get a job on the *AP*," Quigley reminded me. "That's how you were able to get married. Now you've got a wife and child to look after." "Barbara is with me all the way on this," I said. "And she thinks I'll always make enough to provide for our boy. She wants me to do what I can to help Truman because she thinks he's a fine man. My agent, Mary Abbott, believes he can win." He snorted, "What do they know about politics? Haven't they seen the polls? Haven't they read the papers?" "I'm going to take the plunge," I said. Quigley shrugged. "You've had a lot of luck, Frank. Maybe you'll bring some to Harry. I hope you do." "My father and my grandfather were Democrats," I said. "My father always liked Truman. They both served in France in World War I. Maybe I'm hearing a bugle call."

Because of the potato shortage in Ireland in the 1840s, my grandfather Michael Kelly had crossed the ocean to the United States. He settled in Kansas City, where he found the Democrats to be more hospitable to Irish immigrants than the Republicans. My uncle Joseph was active in the Pendergast organization, but he hadn't been involved in any of the corruption. My father had become an executive in the mail order business after he returned from military service—and was a staunch supporter of Franklin Roosevelt and Harry Truman. He was disgusted by the behavior of Tom Pendergast, but he believed the Democratic record was better than that of the Republicans.

My mother and other relatives were Democrats, too, and I knew she would be proud to have me working for Truman. Rose Conway, Truman's personal secretary, was one of her friends. My mother had heard from Miss Conway that Mr. Truman was a gentleman with the highest standards of personal ethics.

Whatever the polls and the newspapers might say, it seemed likely true Democrats would rally behind Truman. I didn't know whether I had the qualifications to put words in a President's mouth, but it seemed to me that I had to give it a try.

I went back down to my apartment and telephoned my wife, feeling a sudden exhilaration. With our two-year-old son, Terry, she was staying with Jerry and Lenore Warwin in Middletown Springs, Vermont. They were friends Barbara had known since her years as a student at Park College. The Warwins were admirers of Henry Wallace, a liberal Democrat they considered to be more progressive than Truman.

"I'm jumping in," I said. "Mary Abbott feels the way you do. She thinks Harry is the right man." "I think you've made the right decision," Barbara said. "Jerry and Lenore are still for Wallace but they hope you

21

can have a good influence on Truman." "I don't know whether I'll have any influence on him at all," I said. "He's going to make two or three hundred speeches. There'll be a whole group pouring ideas into them." "No one else has done a book like yours," Barbara said. "You know words are powerful. Truman knows it, too. You'll think of some lines that he will use."

Barbara and I had been married in December 1941, two days before the Japanese attack on Pearl Harbor. In our seven years together, she had shown more confidence in me than I had in myself. She had persuaded me to apply for a Nieman Fellowship when I didn't think I could get one. That Fellowship had brought me to the attention of Charlie Morton and led to my book contract.

When I had returned from Western Europe in 1945, after my service as a soldier and an army correspondent, I feared I might be sent to the Pacific for the final Allied onslaught against Japan. In the early years of our marriage I had declared I didn't want to bring children into a world torn by war. But I had come close to death several times in Europe and I thought I might be killed if I went to the Pacific. Suddenly I wanted a child, a living descendant, a sign I could be a father, a transmitter of ongoing life. Barbara became pregnant, willing to look after our child if I died in the struggle against Japan.

Then Truman decided to drop atomic bombs in an effort to end the war—and Japan surrendered. I was stationed at Jefferson Barracks near St. Louis when the surrender came. With many of the other men in uniform there, I felt a sense of deliverance. The destruction of two Japanese cities was horrible—but the war itself was the greatest evil. That was over at least. Harry Truman had taken on himself the responsibility for using monstrous weapons to save our lives.

"Quigley thinks I'll be regarded as stupid if I go for Truman," I said. "I guess a lot of people have forgotten the hard decisions he made. But we thought he saved us when the Japanese surrendered." "He saved many lives," Barbara said. "Now you'll have a chance to remind people of what he has done."

I hoped it would go well, but I wondered how I would fit into the group Batt and Birkhead were assembling. "I'm still uneasy about getting into politics," I said. "If MGM had bought my novel, we might have gone to Hollywood. I could be doing more writing." Barbara had kept me from falling into a deep depression after the MGM studios withdrew from negotiations with my agent—after I had been assured they were hot for my novel as a possible movie.

"Some sexy starlet might have tried to take you away from me out there," Barbara said. "Maybe it's more important for you to be battling for Truman." "Aren't there any sexy women in politics?" I teased her. "You're going to be too busy to let any of them catch you," Barbara said. "In any case they can't compete with you," I said. "I'll be home every weekend. You'll have to stay in shape." After I finished talking with Barbara, I felt a warm glow. She was so beautiful and so loving. I hated to be away from her.

Finally I took a long breath and called Bill Batt at the White House. "Can you get here next week?" Batt said. "We're having a meeting in Clifford's office. We've got to move fast." "That sounds fine to me," I answered. "I didn't ask you about the salary or travel arrangements. Could you tell me about that?" "I'll put Kenny on," Batt boomed.

Birkhead came on the line. "Man, you almost missed the boat," he said. "We were just about to call somebody else. As I told you, there'll be five or six of us in the Research Division. We'll be working closely with the White House guys, but there'll be no publicity on what we'll be doing." "Do we have to be cleared by the FBI?" I asked. Birkhead coughed. "No FBI stuff. It's not exactly a hush-hush deal, but there are sensitive people at the National Committee. We'll be part of the Committee but we won't be dealing with the chairman. They might not like it if our direct access to the White House is publicized."

"I've already talked with my agent and others here in New York," I said. "I want you to know that." Birkhead sighed. "If it leaks out, we'll handle it. Quite a few people here already have a little information about it." "I've heard that everything leaks in Washington," I said. "So I won't worry about it. What about salaries and expenses? You know I've got a wife and child. We want to keep our apartment. I suppose I'll have to live in Washington during the week, but I want to get back here on Fridays and Saturdays."

"Each of us will get $8,000 a year, plus a few basic expenses," Birkhead said. "That's not a lot of money but I can get by on it," I said. Our apartment was under New York's rent control law. We paid $45 a month for it, and lived on a careful budget. (In 1948, $8,000 was a fairly decent salary. The cost of living was rising but it hadn't begun to soar rapidly, as it did in subsequent years.)

Birkhead went on, "It's hard to raise money for Truman right now, but the President has some friends who are sending in checks for this project. We have enough to get started, and he'll raise more as we go along. Our salaries end November 1st, and we have no promises of jobs after that." "That tells me what I need to know," I said. "I'm not looking for a job. The Atlantic editors think my book will sell."

"There are some rooms on the top floor of the AVC clubhouse on New Hampshire Avenue available for Research Division guys," Birkhead continued. "Johannes Hoeber, a friend of Batt's, will be staying there, too, and going back to Philadelphia on the weekends. Hoeber is a leader in the Philadelphia reform group. You'll hit it off well with him. He makes puns as bad as yours."

"I'll be there for the meeting next week in Clifford's office," I said. "Will the President be there?" "Clifford says he will be with us," Birkhead said. "I hope Clifford and the President can stand my puns," I warned him. Birkhead laughed. "Batt and I will try to make it clear that you're really a serious guy."

When our conversation ended, I put the telephone receiver back in its cradle. I repressed an urge to call Washington again—to make sure the conversation had been real. Was I actually going to take part in a meeting at the White House? Would I have the nerve to make puns in front of the President and Clark Clifford?

I sat down in the sagging upholstered chair in the bright living room of the apartment. Barbara and I had started our lives together in that apartment. We had romped and laughed in bed there. We had heard a radio announcement on December 7, 1941: "The White House has just reported that Japanese planes have bombed Pearl Harbor." We were just beginning our honeymoon, but I had jumped to the telephone and called the *Associated Press* office in Rockefeller Center. I had been on the *AP* staff for six months then, and thought I might be needed.

Norman Lodge, an editor who had been a soldier in World War I, answered the phone. When I asked him whether I should take a taxi to Rockefeller Center, to give him some help, Lodge snorted "You'll have plenty of time to get into this war, Kelly. Your honeymoon is more important, man. We'll handle the war for a while. You take care of your bride." Barbara forgave me for becoming distracted by the bombing of Pearl Harbor. We turned off the radio and went back to bed. We were sure our love would outlast the war and all the tribulations we might have to endure.

During the presidential campaign of 1944, I had been in Europe as a member of the enormous Allied Expeditionary Force that had crushed the Nazi armies. I had expected Franklin Roosevelt to get re-elected for his fourth term as president. I had not dreamed Roosevelt would die or that Harry Truman would step into the Oval Office.

Remembering the war years, thinking of the tremendous problems Truman faced, I realized that my life had been a series of surprises. I had never planned on being a newspaper man or a war correspondent. I had seen many young men die in Europe before the Allied Victory came. I had landed in Normandy and had participated in the liberation of Paris. I had come home with more health and strength than I had ever enjoyed before.

Perhaps my experience in politics would open new paths and lead me into areas I had never thought about exploring. I walked around my apartment in New York, laughing at my own temerity, wondering whether I could do anything significant for a president who was going to pour a stream of words from one end of the country to another. I had enlisted in a strange struggle—under Harry Truman's banner.

I did hope Truman would carry at least twenty states in November—enough to show my friends I wasn't completely out of my mind when I joined his campaign. If he lost by a landslide, I would try to take it with good humor. I had once written a story—published in a magazine and later in an anthology edited by Edward J. O'Brien—about a desperate young man who retained his sanity by playing a record of triumphant laughter. Through laughter, it was possible to soar beyond the pains of life.

I called Barbara in Vermont once more. The sound of her voice made me believe great things were coming over the horizon. "I'll come up to get you and Terry tomorrow," I said. "I've joined the Truman team, Barbie. I've got to be in Washington next week. If we're going to save Harry and swing the votes, there's no time to lose." "Now that you're on board, I'm sure he's going to win," she responded. "He'll carry thirty states." "Why not thirty-five?" I asked. And then we laughed with sudden joy together.

CHAPTER TWO

WORKING FOR A PRESIDENT WHO DIDN'T KNOW HE COULDN'T WIN

AS I TRAVELED TOWARD WASHINGTON by train on a morning in April 1948, I read articles in newspapers and magazines about Truman's plight—and I wondered how he could keep from sinking into despair when he encountered the barrage of criticisms in those publications. He was depicted as a weak, wobbling leader who had fractured Roosevelt's coalition of progressives, labor unions, big-city machines, and the religious and ethnic groups essential for a Democratic victory. Pundits predicted Truman might not even be nominated at the national convention in July. Prominent Democrats—including two of Roosevelt's sons—were reported to be searching frantically for other candidates.

Those articles chilled me. If Truman didn't get the Democratic nomination, my job wouldn't last long. I felt a surge of gratitude for Charlie Morton, who had obtained an appointment for me on the faculty of Boston University—effective on the day after the votes were counted in November. Morton was positive that the Republicans would win, and he had assured me of getting a position in which I would have time to write books for the Atlantic Monthly Press. He believed that my books would sell very well—in spite of my association with Truman.

When the train reached Washington, I took a taxi to the bank building on Dupont Circle where the Research Division was located. The Democratic National Committee had rented a small suite of rooms there. Bill Batt and Kenny Birkhead greeted me jovially. I shook hands with the other staff members. They were all vigorous young men, full of confidence in themselves and eager to take on their jobs.

I liked all of them. Johannes Hoeber, Batt's friend from Philadelphia, had a sparkling smile. John Barriere, an economist from Chicago, was a tall fellow with a thick shock of hair. Philip Dreyer, a natural resources expert from the Pacific Northwest, was slim and energetic. David Lloyd, a lawyer, had the thoughtful face of a scholar. Batt urged all of us to confront the fact that we had prodigious tasks ahead of us.

The next day, we went to the White House for a long session in Clark Clifford's office. We were taken in through a side entrance, so the reporters in the press room did not know we were there. Clifford apparently did not want to call attention to the mission of the Research Division.

Clifford's office was spacious. He then had the title of Counsel to the President. He was a former naval officer, a lawyer from St. Louis who had gained Truman's respect. He was the chief strategist for the 1948 campaign and one of the most liberal advisors in the White House. In his later years he was a counselor to several presidents, including John Kennedy and Lyndon Johnson.

A tall handsome man with wavy hair, well-dressed and well-groomed, Clark Clifford had the manner of a Washington insider. He thanked Batt for recruiting a talented group of staff members in a difficult time. He indicated that the achievement of a victory in November would require the utmost dedication of every man on board. He asserted that we would have several important assignments—preparing "Files of the Facts" on the urgent issues facing the country, outlining ways in which the President would deal with those facts, and drafting speeches for Mr. Truman's use on his trips throughout the nation. He promised us that our ideas and suggestions would be invited at all times, and would be carefully considered by him and by the President.

Batt then gave each of us a memorandum dated April 5, 1948, headed: "Research Division Functions." We were asked to study it and refer to it as the basic outline for our activities. It was not signed, and I did not learn whether Clifford or Batt or George Elsey (another one of Truman's assistants) had written it. But it was evident that Clifford was the man who had persuaded the President to establish the Research Division as a fundamental instrument for Truman's campaign.

It did not strike me as strange that all the members of the campaign group were men. I did not expect to find any women in Truman's inner circle. I knew he was devoted to his wife, Bess, and his daughter, Margaret, but he did not have any female consultants on his staff. In his time, few women were openly active in national politics.

Eleanor Roosevelt, the late president's wife, wrote a newspaper column and voiced her views on every issue. She had played an important role in the development and extension of the New Deal. But Mrs. Truman was not comfortable in politics and she did not enjoy the atmosphere in Washington.

I participated in that meeting because two women had convinced me Truman was the right man to lead the country. I learned later Bill Batt's wife, Jane, was an enthusiastic advocate of Truman's program. Birkhead's wife—another Barbara—had a major impact on his thinking. Charlotte Lloyd, David's spouse, was an impressive person. I was sure women had been influential in shaping the lives of all the men there.

After we had received copies of the "Research Division" outline, Clifford introduced two Democratic leaders from the Middle West who were extremely gloomy. They were doubtful Truman could overcome the negative feelings that had arisen among voters in Iowa, Missouri, and Nebraska. They blamed the press, which printed many articles about Truman's inability to get his proposals enacted by the Republican Congress.

"There is very little we can do about the press," Clifford said. "But the President can reach the people when he goes through those areas on his train." "We hope so," one of the men said. While he was speaking in a skeptical tone, we heard quick footsteps. President Truman came swiftly into the room. We stood up and he greeted each of us with a few words.

When Truman met with us that day, he indicated that he recalled my father's combat service as an infantry captain in the 89th Division in France in 1918. He was aware of what infantry soldiers went through in that war. He had been an artillery captain but he had not engaged in the hand-to-hand combat in the bloody trenches. He said he appreciated my father's support in his previous campaigns.

His bright blue eyes radiated cordiality and confidence. He looked straight into me. He gave me a feeling of security, a sense of steady friendship. I learned later the crucial decisions he had been required to make—especially the smashing of two Japanese cities with atomic bombs—had caused him a great deal of inner suffering. But he believed that a man had to shoulder whatever responsibilities fell upon him—and should not reveal the anguish that would always be with him.

Perhaps I was affected by the atmosphere of the White House, but it seemed to me Harry Truman walked with the air of a man who had dismissed the idea he could be beaten by his enemies. I had wondered whether he would show signs of having his back to a wall, but I couldn't detect the slightest sign he was disheartened by any of the attacks launched again him. He made a light remark about my years on the *Kansas City Star*—that solidly Republican paper, which denounced and demeaned him on many occasions. Roy Roberts, the *Star*'s managing editor, was one of his worst critics.

I was astonished by the exhilaration that went through me in Truman's presence. I had met Roosevelt once, and had felt the power of F.D.R.'s majestic strength. Truman didn't have that kingly manner, but he was evidently a man in command of himself and ready to meet any situation. Whatever happened, I knew it was an honor to be one of Sir Harry's lieutenants. Truman sat down in a chair next to Clifford's desk. He turned to the men from the Middle West and spoke briskly, "Go on with your reports, boys, and don't pull any punches."

"You've got an uphill fight where we come from," one of them said. Clifford nodded. "We're in trouble in the farming counties. We knew that." The men shook their heads. "It's worse than trouble. They are really down on you, Mr. President."

"That's because of Republican propaganda," Truman snapped. "We'll show them that we've got a better farm program than the Republicans can offer them." "We hope you can get it across," the man near me muttered glumly. Truman leaned toward him. "Don't you worry about it. I've been a farmer myself. I'll talk straight to them. We'll carry those counties before we are through. Tom Dewey doesn't know a damned thing about farming. I do." "You've proved that," Clifford said.

Truman made a chopping gesture with his right hand. "Now, boys, let me tell you something. Don't be a bit fazed by these bad reports.

People said I was down and out in 1940. The pundits didn't think I could keep my seat in the Senate then. I won. I won with Roosevelt in '44. We're going to win this year, too. Don't ever doubt it." The men from the Middle West stared at the carpet and shrugged their shoulders. Watching them, I realized Truman had not removed their pessimism. But I also realized he meant what he had told them. He wasn't about to be licked by Tom Dewey or anybody else.

The President rose from his chair and walked toward the door. "I've got to get back to my desk," he said. "I have a lot of work to do. So do you, boys. We'll have to put in some long hours." Then he wheeled around and beamed at us. His eyes sparkled behind his glasses and I saw he was actually full of joy. He was a man of peace, but he relished a good fight.

"We're going to surprise people," Truman said. "I'll go across this country from one end to the other, and I'll give people the facts about our problems and what we can do about them. They'll understand that I know what I'm talking about. We won't be peddling any baloney. Facts—that's what people want, boys, and that's what we'll give them." He made a sweeping gesture with his right hand. "Henry Wallace and Strom Thurmond won't get very far. The Republicans are going to nom-inate Tom Dewey, and the voters will see that Dewey is a phony. I'm not. People don't want a phony in the White House." Then the President smiled and snapped his fingers, saying, "I'll take Dewey like that!"

After Truman left the room, there was a moment of silence. "He's a man who doesn't think he can be defeated," Clifford said. "I hope he's right again." One of the men from the Middle West spoke, "He has done some big things. But people don't rate him as high as Roosevelt." "They'll see him as higher than Dewey," Bill Batt said. "Or Wallace or Thurmond. He doesn't have to be another Roosevelt." "Roosevelt asked him to be on the ticket in 1944," I said. "That counts with me. It counts for all of us who thought F.D.R. was the greatest president we ever had."

In the process of doing my book about Truman's confrontation with Stalin over the future of Iran, I had begun to understand why Roosevelt had accepted Truman as a running mate in 1944. Truman had the inner strength essential for a president in crucial situations.

Face-to-face with Truman that day in the White House, I was keenly aware I was in the presence of an extraordinary human being. I understood why my friend, Joe Guilfoyle, who had been on Truman's staff in the Senate, had such respect for him. Guilfoyle had assured me Truman was better educated than most of the college graduates on Capitol Hill. Truman had read the histories of many countries and carried a visionary poem by Alfred Tennyson in his wallet. Truman was generous to his staff and kind to every one he met.

I knew Truman worked day and night to meet the demands of his position. In hours of relaxation with his friends, he enjoyed earthy stories, Wild Turkey bourbon whisky, and games of low-stakes poker. He regarded himself as a citizen who happened to be the Chief Executive of the United States. He did not think his status entitled him to be pompous or arrogant.

Some of my friends viewed him as a man with innocent blood on his hands, because he had authorized the dropping of atomic bombs. Truman had publicly declared he had made that horrible decision to end a terrible war and so to save many thousands of lives. I accepted his explanation. I had been in that war and I believed he had done what he had to do.

On that day in Clark Clifford's office, I saw he was a gifted man, a very bright man, crackling with energy and determination, a man who carried the weight of the presidency as well as any man could, a man who kept his internal anguish to himself. He presented himself as a man better qualified for that job than any of his opponents. I felt that he could convince many people he was right.

After the meeting was over, I rode in a taxi with Batt and Birkhead to the bank building on Dupont Circle. The tree-lined streets of Washington gleamed in the April sun. The fragrant air of spring was delightful. I was glad to be there.

As we climbed the stairs to the second floor of the building, I was suddenly stunned by the range of duties Truman and Clifford had placed upon the members of the Research Division. "I didn't expect to have the President and his men load so much on us," I said. Batt slapped me on the back. "Doesn't that make you feel good, man? The whole campaign may depend on us. I don't believe a group of this kind has ever been put together for a presidential candidate before. We're making history, Kelly." "Win or lose," Birkhead said. "We're going to win," Batt insisted. "Do you think a guy with Truman's strength can lose?"

Batt went down a corridor to his office. Birkhead and I went into the cubicle to which we had been assigned. Our desks were side by side. It was a narrow, stuffy room. "If we're making history in here, let's open a window," I said. Birkhead got the window open. Pile drivers for a construction project were pounding away in Dupont Circle, but the air was fresh. Birkhead said, "I told you Truman is struggling to raise money. The President had to do some begging to get us this." "And beggars can't be choosers," I said. "And with those pile drivers going, we'll turn out some hard-hitting stuff."

Batt appeared in the doorway behind Birkhead. His laughter resounded from the thin walls of the cubicle. Behind our desks were several file cabinets. There was an old standard typewriter on my desk and one on Birkhead's. There were stacks of yellow folders on each desk. "Those folders are full of stuff from government agencies," Batt said. "The White House can pull anything it wants from any agency. Let them know what you need and they'll get it for you. We're going to have facts running out of our ears."

"As the President told us, he likes speeches packed with facts," Birkhead reminded me. "We'll offer suggestions for his major speeches, and probably some drafts. But we'll mainly concentrate on the short ones—the five to ten minute talks he'll give from the back platform of his train."

"Will we get to ride on the train?" I asked. Batt rubbed his chin. "I don't think so. We'll send our stuff to George Elsey and Clark Clifford and Charlie Murphy. They'll be traveling with Truman." "Too bad," I said. "I like trains." "This is more important than being on the train," Batt said. "We'll be giving Truman stuff he can use all over the country. And put together in short, snappy sentences. That's what Truman likes."

33

"Next to trains, I like short sentences," I said. Batt nodded. "Sentences that pack a punch. We want to put at least one crackling line in every speech. We're expecting you to produce some of those lines, Kelly." "How many a day?" I asked, grinning. "What's my quota?" "No quotas," Batt said. "The best you've got, that's all. See you later." He left the room and I stared at Birkhead. "I hope I can produce what he wants. You must have given me a big build-up."

When I had gone to the University of Kansas City, I had shared a deep interest with Birkhead: We both loved music—all kinds of music. We listened to Beethoven and Brahms at Saturday night sessions in the apartment of Clarence Decker, one of our professors. We also exulted in the lively rhythms of Cab Calloway, Duke Ellington, Benny Moten, and other jazz musicians. Kansas City was a hot town for jazz in the 1930s.

"When we were sitting in those night clubs, listening to the trumpets and saxophones, I never imagined we'd be here in Washington, trying to help a president who's supposed to be a sure loser," I said. "He's not a sure loser," Birkhead said, taking off his coat. He opened the door of a narrow closet and put his coat on a hanger. "Nobody can beat him. We're lucky to get in on this."

I put my coat in the closet, rolled up my shirtsleeves, pulled out a stack of papers from a folder, and started my service as a back-room ghost for Truman. Birkhead had given me a sheaf of reports on the housing situation in the country. After I had left the *AP* in 1946, I had been an information specialist for the National Housing Agency, created by President Roosevelt and supported by the Truman administration.

"Bill would like to have you try your hand at several speeches about the housing problems," Birkhead said. "The President is going to hit hard on the bad record of the Republican Congress. They've sabotaged the housing program." "I know they have," I said. "The Housing Agency was kicked around when I was there. That's why I left."

The reports I pulled from the folder indicated that five million families were living in slums. Another four million had to live in decaying houses and apartment buildings neededing repairs. Three million families were doubled up in crowded quarters with other families—including veterans who could not afford new homes. "These reports make my blood pressure rise," I said. "Providing decent places to live ought to be one of the main points in Truman's campaign." "I think it will be," Birkhead agreed. "Along with his efforts for peace and his fight against inflation."

"Peace, prices, and places to live." I rose from my chair. "As your President, I promise you we will avoid war, we will control prices, and we will build millions of houses. I will strive by day and by night to carry out those promises...." Birkhead chuckled. "Don't make a speech to me," he said. "Get your ideas down on paper. Then we'll send them to Elsey, Clifford and Murphy, and they'll give the President the best ones you produce."

I sat down again. I realized that writing drafts of speeches for a president was very different from turning out news stories for the *Star* or the *AP*. Every speech had to be packed with facts—but it also had to be seasoned with stinging words. Truman believed that the power of words, delivered with fiery energy, could awaken people from their lethargy, change their minds, turn them around.

When I had joined the campaign staff, I had been enormously confident of my abilities. Almost everything I had written for newspapers and magazines had been published. My book had been accepted with enthusiasm. So I was sure I could whip up political speeches on any theme with a minimum of sweat. In fact, I regarded such speeches as a low form of literary activity. When I didn't begin to type, Birkhead interrupted my reverie. "In your science fiction stories, did you ever imagine you were on a President's staff?" "No," I said. "I didn't anticipate anything like this."

In the 1930s I had produced a stream of fantastic tales about adventures in outer space and distant times, projecting many possibilities into the future. In one story I had anticipated a possible war between the United States and the Soviet Union. In another, I had written about a Japanese attack on the United States, supposedly occurring in 1940. I did not know where those ideas came from, or why I had been able to sell them to magazines. I had leaped easily from planet to planet.

But when I sat in that little office in Washington, I began to wonder

35

whether I was in the right place at the right time. Was I prepared to do what I was expected to do? Were any of the men in the Research Division or on the White House staff really qualified to pour streams of words into the mind of a President who would be speaking to citizens in all parts of the country on a huge range of topics? No one had given us an examination on what experience or wisdom had made us eligible for such demanding assignments.

Many of the citizens who would listen to Truman's words would not be well enough informed to ask sensible questions. Many of them were likely to be confused, swayed by false statements in the mass media, skeptical about themselves and their leaders, uncertain of their own responsibilities, unclear about what they wanted for themselves and coming generations. The information and ideas we gathered and dispatched to the men on Truman's train would affect their decisions as voters in November of that year—and the repercussions would be felt in these times and in the decades ahead.

Then I heard the sound of Birkhead's typewriter. He was pounding away at a memorandum or a draft of a speech. Whether I was qualified or not, I knew I had to get going. So I did.

I had no idea then that I was changing my identity. By committing myself to Truman and his program, I was no longer a freelance writer selecting what I would write about and what I would do with the pages I produced. In my year with the housing agency I had focused my attention on certain topics and I had become saturated with information about the needs of people seeking homes for themselves and their families. But I had not been labeled as "a housing reporter" and I had not identified myself with that agency. I had written articles on other subjects and I didn't feel that my whole future would be shaped by my work in that field.

In that small office, I tried to think like a President. I visualized the people who would be standing around the train when Harry Truman appeared before them as their elected leader. I was sure that they would expect him to be blunt and down to earth. But they also would hope for some inspiration—for flashes of awareness that their President was more than a common man who had been installed in his office by the bosses of the Democratic party. They would hope to hear things they could tell their neighbors—stories they might remember as long as they lived.

While I was putting words on paper and throwing them into a wastebasket—and trying again to get the right words in the right order—I had a brief vision of my mother, praying for me. In every letter she sent to me from Kansas City, she assured me that she was praying for me—and for Barbara and for our son, Terry. She knew I didn't say the prayers she had taught me when I was a child; she knew that I had become a skeptic, a man who questioned everything. She knew she had to do the praying I wouldn't do.

I also became aware of the encouraging presence of my wife, who was almost always in my mind. I felt she knew I was struggling to do something powerful, something memorable, something great enough to be a truly presidential utterance. And I was thankful then for the help I was getting, for the grace I was receiving from people who loved me and cared about what I faced.

I knew Barbara was full of grace. When I had met her at the home of friends in Kansas City, I saw she was spiritually beautiful as well as physically attractive. She was a musician, a pianist, a woman with a vibrant voice; she sang in the choir of St. Andrew's church in Kansas City. When she accepted my proposal and came to New York to marry me, she called the former rector of that church—James De Wolfe—and he agreed to do our wedding service in a chapel of the Cathedral of St. John the Divine. He had become dean of the Cathedral.

Barbara had never lost her faith in God, as I had. She was a poet, a reader of Shakespeare, Dante, and William Blake. She believed Shakespeare was inspired when he wrote these words for Hamlet: "There's a divinity that shapes our ends, rough-hew them how we will." She was sure I would eventually recognize the power of God in all the changes of my life—in the decisions I made, in the responses I gave to the demands upon me.

When I started my work as a member of Truman's campaign staff that day in Washington—listening to the slam and bang of the pile drivers outside, trying to hit hard with what I wrote—I didn't know Harry Truman had a favorite prayer. I learned about it later, when I studied his life and his development as a leader. The prayer emphasized honesty, kindness and a full understanding of the motives and actions of himself and other human beings: "Oh Almighty and Everlasting God, creator of Heaven, Earth and the Universe: Help me to be, to think, to act what is right, because it is right: make me truthful, honest and honorable in all things: make me intellectually honest for the sake of right and honor and without thought of reward to me. Give me the ability to be charitable, forgiving and patient with my fellow men—help me to understand their motives and their shortcomings—even as Thou understandest mine. Amen, amen, amen."

In the heat of the struggle in 1948, I hammered out statements about the Republicans that were not charitable or forgiving. I questioned their motives—and Truman used some of my stinging lines.

Since Truman had recorded that prayer in his diary—and it became known to historians—it is likely he offered it to the Almighty during the blazing months of his battle for the presidency. He was not able to be totally forgiving to those who denounced and attacked him from the right and from the left, but he undoubtedly begged God to keep him from making nasty replies. He refused to make harsh statements about their personal behavior.

All of us in the Research Division felt we were justified in expressing our anger against the reactionary Republicans who had tried to destroy the progressive laws which had been passed under the leadership of Roosevelt and Truman. We were delighted when Truman lambasted them in villages, towns and cities across the country.

CHAPTER THREE

*TRUMAN ON THE ROAD, AROUSING THE PEOPLE
AND SURPRISING THE PRESS*

WHEN TRUMAN LEFT WASHINGTON the evening of June 3 for his first journey on his "Presidential Special," he took with him eighteen members of his staff, his Secret Service guards, and dozens of reporters and photographers. Clifford, Elsey, Murphy, and others on board the train had briefcases filled with ideas, facts, suggestions and speech-drafts from the Research Division, as well as particular information about the cities and towns along his route from the capital to California. No one from our Division was in the presidential party, but our thoughts were with him.

Truman walked to his armor-plated Pullman car with a jaunty stride. He had been invited to receive an honorary degree from the University of California at Berkeley—and to deliver a commencement speech there. He had never gone to a university, but he was confident that the students and faculty members (and their families and friends) would be interested in what he planned to tell them about the state of the world.

In the "Files of the Facts" we had prepared for the President, we had noted that the period after the Allied victory in World War II had not been the time of peace and security which the victors had expected to achieve. The "cold war" struggle between the Western nations and the Soviet bloc had begun soon after the defeat of the Nazis and the Japanese militarists. The Soviets had refused to participate in the Marshall Plan—the European Recovery Program initiated by Truman and his advisors. Stalin had feared that the plan would lead to the domination of Eastern Europe and the Soviet Union by the capitalist countries. Determined to control most of Germany, the Soviets had tried to squeeze the American, British, and French forces out of Berlin.

In spite of the perilous situation in Europe and the other problems he faced on that night in June, Truman was exhilarated by the prospect of getting away from Washington and talking with thousands of people from coast to coast. He had retained his place in the Senate in 1940— when political experts predicted his defeat—by face-to-face campaigning. He thought he could carry the country by the same means in 1948.

The President was delighted by the number of people who gathered around his train when he made a stop at noon on June 4 in the small town of Crestline, Ohio. A thousand persons had assembled there to welcome him. Members of the campaign staff had telephoned Democrats and urged them to give him a big round of applause. When the crowd cheered virtually everything he said, Truman joked about his "nonpartisan, bipartisan trip" and noted gleefully: "I understand there are a whole lot of Democrats present ...." He waved his arms with the exuberance of a man who had been released from the confinement of the executive mansion in Washington.

"The President, you know, is virtually in jail," Truman asserted. "He goes from his study to his office and from his office to his study, and he has to have guards there all the time." He added, "When you go out and see people and find out what people are thinking about, you can do a better job...."

In Chicago, when he rode from the railroad station to the Palmer House in an open car, he was applauded by 100,000 people who filled the streets. In Omaha, Nebraska, supposedly a Republican city, he marched with men from the 35th Army Division. As he stepped along at a rapid pace with members of his old Artillery Battery D, thousands of citizens clapped and yelled shouts of encouragement to him.

Edward T. Folliard described the scene in a dispatch to the *Washington Post*: "They lined the streets in this Republican stronghold, 160,000 of them, and gave President Truman a welcome reminiscent of his 'honeymoon' days in the White House three years ago." Folliard and other reporters noted the affection expressed for Truman there.

But Truman received a shock when he arrived at the Ak-Sar-Ben Auditorium to give a major speech that night. The auditorium had been rented by veterans of the 35th Division, who were having a reunion in Omaha. In the publicity for that event, no mention had been made of the fact that the gathering was open to the public. Fewer than 2,000 persons were in the huge hall—and 8,000 seats were empty.

Photographs of those thousands of empty seats appeared in newspapers across the nation—and commentators promptly interpreted the pictures to mean that Truman was still at a low ebb in popularity. But Truman wasn't downhearted about the incident. His speech had been broadcast by radio stations in Nebraska—and he knew he had reached tens of thousands of farmers with his attack on the Republican 80th Congress.

As he approached the West Coast his blasts at the Republicans became more explosive. In Bremerton, Washington, he declared: "You know, this Congress is interested in the welfare of the better classes. They are not interested in the welfare of the common everyday man." A man near the train shouted: "Pour it on, Harry!" "I'm going to," Truman answered quickly. "I'm going to."

In Olympia, Washington, he chided the voters who were responsible for the election of the Republican majority in 1946. He advised the people, "Educate yourselves. You don't want to do like you did in 946. Two-thirds of you stayed home in 1946, and look at what a Congress we got! That is your fault!"

When he told a reporter he regarded the 80th Congress as the worst in the history of the United States, Republican legislators denounced him in bitter terms. House Majority Leader Charles Halleck labeled Truman as the worst President in history, and Representative Cliff Clevenger of Ohio sneered at him as "a nasty little gamin" and a "Missouri jackass." Truman brushed off their statements and went on lashing "the Republican record."

In Berkeley, California, 55,000 people came to the university's football stadium to hear him deliver one of his most eloquent addresses. It was carried by radio stations across the nation. In the Research Division office in Washington, we listened to that speech with a growing appreciation for Truman's stature as a global statesman.

"Our policy will continue to be a policy of recovery, reconstruction, prosperity—and peace with freedom and justice," Truman said. He declared that the United States was not interested in extending its power by force. Attempting to reassure the Russians, he expressed his belief that different economic systems could live together on earth without military conflicts if neither side tried to destroy the other.

"The only expansion we are interested in is the expansion of human freedom and the wider enjoyment of the good things of the earth in all countries," Truman told the enormous crowd of students, faculty members, and people from many backgrounds who had assembled to hear him. "The only realm in which we aspire to eminence exists in the minds of men, where authority is exercised through the qualities of sincerity, compassion and right conduct. The only prize we covet is the respect and good will of our fellow members of the family of nations."

All of the seven men in the Research Division had contributed phrases, ideas, sentences, and suggestions for the speeches Truman delivered on his trip to California. Bill Batt, Kenny Birkhead, Phil Dreyer, and I were members of the American Veterans Committee. We knew the horrible effects of war. While we regarded the Soviet Union as a dangerous nation, we believed that a policy of 'peaceful co-existence' between the United States and the Communist empire had to be maintained. We were confident that the Soviets could be blocked without the carnage of a military struggle.

When Truman asserted that "the only realm in which we aspire to eminence exists in the minds of men," he made us proud to be serving under his banner. The Soviets—and some of his critics in Congress—accused him of wanting to dominate the world. But we were sure that he had no such ambition. He wanted to win "the respect and good will" of the people in all nations by aiding them to develop societies flourishing in an atmosphere of freedom.

Truman and his staff members were amazed and invigorated by the throng he encountered in Los Angeles on June 14. Police estimated that a million people lined the streets to watch him ride from the railroad station to the Ambassador Hotel. The *Los Angeles Times* reported: "They clung to the roofs of buildings, jammed windows and fire escapes, and crowded five deep along the sidewalk."

In a speech at the Press Club, the President again derided the Republican Congress. He excoriated the legislators for refusing to act on his proposals for price controls, a national housing program, farm supports, health insurance, and an extension of the Social Security program. He had vetoed a Republican bill which would have removed 750,000 people from the Social Security rolls. He demanded action on a bill for federal aid to education which had been passed by the Senate and stymied in the House.

That first trip from Washington to California crackled with the intensity of Truman's drive to arouse the people—to get his fellow citizens to accept their responsibilities for the future of their country and the future of humanity. He traveled 9,505 miles, spoke to people in 18 states, made 73 speeches on a wide array of topics, and was glimpsed by several million citizens. Many of them were in towns never visited by a President before. Much of the information for his speeches was drawn from state guidebooks prepared by the Works Progress Administration (WPA), created by Congress in 1935 at the urging of President Roosevelt.

The enthusiastic receptions given to Truman in dozens of places did not diminish the cockiness of the Republican leaders. When the Republican national convention held its opening session in Philadelphia on June 21—three days after Truman returned to Washington—Clare Boothe Luce (a former member of Congress, wife of Henry Luce, publisher of *Time* and *Life*) assured the prosperous and complacent delegates that Harry Truman was "a gone goose." The delegates gave her an ovation. In the White House, the "gone goose" watched some of the Republican antics on a small television screen. He told staff members with a smile: "They're going to be surprised."

On June 24, the Republicans nominated Governor Thomas E. Dewey of New York as their presidential candidate and Governor Earl Warren of California as his running mate. Dewey had waged a strong fight against Franklin Roosevelt in 1944, and Warren was admired for his policies in California. The Dewey-Warren ticket was rated by political observers as the best combination for a Republican landslide. *Time* and *Newsweek* carried articles indicating it would take a miracle for Truman to avoid a crushing defeat.

The President didn't spend much time worrying about Dewey or Warren. He was confronted by a crisis in Europe. The Soviets tightened their hold on Berlin. The sectors controlled by the Western Allies were deprived of access to food, fuel, and other supplies. General Clay, the American commander in Berlin, estimated that two and a half million people would be starving within a month. Clay had begun to bring in some supplies by air but he was doubtful about the abilities of the Allies to mount a massive airlift.

Truman rejected a proposal to send an armored column to break the Soviet blockade. He didn't want to provoke an immediate battle. After meetings with his cabinet members and the Joint Chiefs of Staff, he ordered the creation of an around-the-clock operation by planes to sustain the people and the Allied troops in Western Berlin. No one knew whether the Allied forces could maintain such an airlift long enough to overcome the Soviet blockade.

After it became clear the airlift was a tremendous achievement, I asked Truman how he had made his decision to authorize it. He grinned and told me he had simply followed his mother's advice, just as he did in other situations. "The military boys informed me we were in a bad position," Truman said. "They weren't sure we should try to stay in Berlin. They thought the Soviets might make a move somewhere else, after we had lined up all those planes for Berlin. General Vandenberg, the chief of the air force, was troubled about that. I understood how he felt."

Truman went on: "I asked those boys—you know, the Joint Chiefs of Staff—if we had a right to be in Berlin. They agreed with me we had a right to be there. Then I told them I would take full responsibility for the airlift. I quoted my mother. I said she instructed me to do what was right and take the consequences." As I listened to him, I thought I could understand how startled the Chiefs of Staff must have been to receive orders from a President who explained that he was obeying his mother.

Three women were highly influential in Truman's life—his mother, his wife, and his daughter. On his campaign trips in 1948 Truman frequently introduced his wife to his audiences, calling her "the Boss." She didn't like that title and she chided him for using it, but it was evident to his staff members that he often deferred to her. He had fallen in love with her in a Sunday School class and his love was enduring.

Truman knew that women had enough votes to swing the election for him. When he delivered speeches aimed at women, however, he did not make pleas on his own behalf. He asked them to use their power "to bring about a secure and good future for yourselves and your families." He praised them for their devotion to "the arts of peace," saying that women had discovered "ways of making peace exciting and full of challenge."

Although he didn't have any women in his cabinet, Truman had appointed women as delegates to UNESCO and the United Nations Commission on the Status of Women. In an address to a conference of women leaders, he declared that "there should be monuments to the successes" of women in many fields. He urged women's organizations to use their power to push legislation through Congress providing for "equal pay for equal work" and "the ending of specific discriminations against women." He asked women to accept special responsibilities in the struggle "against poverty and fear and disease and hunger."

In Truman's view, no one was more important in shaping the characters of human beings than the mothers who raised families. He referred to them as "home makers" and he asserted in his talks that he shared their concerns about rising prices and "the proper schooling of children."

On my trips to New York—which I made every Friday to be with Barbara and my two-year-old son, Terry—I learned that Truman's forthrightness and his advocacy of federal programs for aid to education, a national health plan, and other ideas registered well with the women I knew. Barbara and Mary Abbott, my literary agent, commented on Truman's effective speeches. Mrs. Abbott thought he was gaining ground among the people she encountered.

But I was often depressed by what I read in the New York tabloids— the *Daily News* and the *Mirror*—which contained articles sniping at Truman or treating him as a subject for jokes. Some of our friends were determined to support Henry Wallace and others warned me Truman would probably wreck the Democratic Party if he got the presidential nomination at the July convention. They feared he would bring many senators and representatives down to defeat with him.

My Saturdays and Sundays with Barbara and Terry refreshed me. We walked in Washington Square Park or rode uptown on the double-deck buses to museums and art galleries. Barbara was writing poems that stirred and shook me. She was an increasingly radiant and beautiful woman, full of laughter and love. Terry astonished me by his rapid development. He was fascinated by everything—eager to talk and play games, eager to wake us up when we overslept in the mornings, eager to explore the city around him.

The days were golden and the nights were balmy during that summer of 1948. New York was exciting but not frenzied. It seemed to be safe to walk through the streets during the day and at night. The headlines on the papers indicated that another war might be imminent and voices on the radio stations spoke of an approaching crisis, but there were no signs of panic.

Sometimes I awoke in the night, thinking of what could happen to Barbara and Terry if another war occurred. I had wanted a child so deeply that I had pushed aside my knowledge of the terrible dangers faced by every human being—by every living creature—in a world shadowed by the existence of nuclear bombs. I had enlisted in the campaign of a man who had authorized the use of such bombs on two cities.

Yet, I believed Truman had been convinced the bombs would bring a quick ending to the Pacific war. I believed that he hated war and would do everything possible to avoid another one. He spoke bluntly to the Soviets but he never broke off negotiations with them. I felt reassured when I remembered how he had handled the crisis of 1946, when the Soviets seemed to be determined to maintain their occupation of northern Iran. In the end, a peaceful settlement had been reached.

Tremendous changes were occurring in the world. There was no way for me to provide absolute security for my wife and my child. I had to depend on the intelligence of the political leaders of the nations, who were aware of what destruction a war might bring upon them. I trusted

Truman. He had been in combat zones in World War II. He had been personally affected by the deaths of many people in that horrifying struggle.

I went back to Washington each week to serve under Truman's banner. I was glad that he emphasized three themes in his speeches: "Peace, prices, and places to live!" Those were the vital issues for many men and women in my generation. As a veteran, I knew how much the participants in World War II—and their families—wanted peace. As a middle-class citizen, I knew how the rising costs of food, clothing and other necessities strained family budgets. I realized how many people were trying to save enough money to buy affordable homes.

When Truman was on the road, his attacks on the Republican Congress had drawn enthusiastic responses from crowds. The Congress had adjourned for the summer, but the President had the power to summon it for a special session. In the Research Division, we drafted a memorandum entitled: "Should the President call Congress back?" We outlined arguments for and against such an action. Theoretically, a President was not supposed to force a Congress to return to Washington in order to demonstrate his leadership and enhance his standing with the voters. Special sessions were expected to be rare events dealing with very important issues.

In our offices on Dupont Circle we debated whether a special session would be beneficial to Harry Truman or to the Republican leaders on Capitol Hill. There was a possibility that Senator Robert Taft would come up with a series of legislative ideas and try to overshadow Truman's program. If Congress didn't act on any of the President's major proposals, the President would be depicted in the press as ineffectual and unable to get anything done.

But we finally decided that the calling of that session would be worth whatever risks might be involved. It would show the people that Truman was trying to get a recalcitrant Congress to deal with the problems of the country.

Batt presented the idea to a gathering of Truman's advisors, but it was turned down. When he reported this to us in the Research Division, we felt it should not be dropped. Batt then presented our arguments for it to Clark Clifford, who took it to the President with his endorsement. My support for the special session was based partly on disgust at the treatment given Truman by many newspapers. Truman was often depicted as a desperate candidate,swinging wildly at his opponents. The constructive substance in his speeches seldom got the extensive coverage it deserved.

In 1946, I had collaborated with other Nieman Fellows at Harvard to produce a book called *Your Newspaper*. As professional journalists we pointed out the deficiencies of the press in many fields. Our own experience had given us examples of how the articles in daily papers—including such notable ones as the *New York Times*, the *Philadelphia Bulletin*, and the *Chicago Tribune*—were often flawed or superficial.

The whole Truman campaign was designed as a communications plan which enabled the President to reach the people directly. His opponents scoffed at the small towns in which his train halted while Truman spoke crisply. The towns were labeled "whistle stops." But Truman realized that the crowds which came to hear him talked to their neighbors about what they had heard—and spread the word about his statements from town to town.

In the months between June and November 1948, few newspapers attempted to convey to their readers what Truman was really saying to the people. Few editors were aware of the range of information provided to the President by those of us who spent our days and nights in sending a stream of facts and ideas to his train. Only the *New York Times* printed an article on the existence of the Research Division and its relationships to Truman's hundreds of speeches.

Although Truman was skeptical about public opinion polls, we found that a survey conducted by Elmo Roper was extremely useful in revealing what many Americans considered to be the most important concerns in their lives. Incomes and savings had gone up steadily during the war years, but citizens were worried about a possible depression. The removal of price controls by the Congress had released a surge of inflation—and people were angry about the declining value of the dollar. People wanted the nation to be strong enough to meet any emergency, but they feared the rising strength of the Soviets. We prepared materials dealing with all of those issues.

In an article he wrote later for the *Presidential Studies Quarterly*, Batt declared: "Were it not for Clifford's good judgment, it would probably have died on his desk. Truman seized upon the idea. In effect, the President said to the Republicans, 'put your money where your mouth is.' Since the whole campaign was based upon running against Congress, the idea fit into the campaign's strategy like a hand into a glove."

We did not participate in the conversation Clifford had with the President, but we heard later that Truman was not disturbed by the possibility of cooperation between Senator Taft and Governor Dewey in getting the Republican Congress to act on the proposals in the Republican platform. Truman knew the two men did not get along very well. Taft would not be inclined to try to push any measure through the Senate at a special session.

While the proposal for a recall of Congress was being developed, we continued to produce drafts of speeches for the President's campaign appearances. We sent suggestions to the White House staff for Truman's use in preparing the speech he would give when he accepted the presidential nomination.

Bill Batt asked me to go to Philadelphia to assist the committee, which was striving to put together the Democratic Platform—a document designed to present the case for the Democratic Party in 1948. I was reluctant to take that assignment. I knew the Committee was deeply divided between the liberals and the conservatives. The members had many years of experience in politics. I doubted they would listen to anyone from the Research Division.

Batt assured me I would be sent there with the backing of the White House. He said the President would be in close touch with the Committee—and would personally review each section of the platform. Truman did not regard it as merely a rhetorical exercise. My job would be to keep the members aware of the President's interest and to try to make sure that each section reflected Truman's views clearly and emphatically. In spite of all the dissension in the Party, it was very likely that Truman would be the presidential nominee—and he wanted the Platform to be one he could run on without any reservations.

So I went to the steaming city of Philadelphia—knowing I would not find it to be a City of Brotherly Love but a city in which angry Democrats would confront one another. I was given a place at a long table in a smoky hotel room where various parts of the platform were drafted, dissected, reassembled, revised and reluctantly accepted. I sat next to a smiling young lawyer named Alfred Vigderman, an assistant to Scott Lucas of Illinois, who was then the Democratic Whip in the Senate.

Vigderman and I soon found we had many things in common—including our desires to fill the platform with bold statements on the policies we thought the country should adopt. We sharpened our wits in arguments with other committee staff members and we became friends within a few days. We thought of ourselves as sophisticated young men—readers of *The New Yorker* and *Esquire*—who had to put some bright touches to the pedestrian language of the professional politicians around us.

We wondered whether a "platform"—a carefully concocted collection of statements on the principles and achievements of a political party—would be thoughtfully weighed by the millions of confused voters who called themselves Democrats or Republicans or "independents." We realized that many of those voters—like ourselves—had read enough history to remember that winning candidates often jettisoned platforms after their victories had been won.

Yet, we were convinced the election of 1948 was a crucial one, particularly for members of our generation who regarded Roosevelt's New Deal as essential for the economic and spiritual health of the nation and the world. We supported Truman because he had fought under Roosevelt's banner and had demonstrated his basic commitment to the liberal principles to which we were dedicated. We felt we had to do everything we could to remind the people of what had been achieved since 1933—and what might be lost if the Democratic candidates were beaten in November.

Taking part in the drafting of that platform widened my understanding of the enormous complexities of American politics. And my friendship with Al Vigderman, formed in the clouded atmosphere in Philadelphia, eventually led to my participation in the fight for Truman's program during my years as a chief assistant to two Majority Leaders of the United States Senate.

CHAPTER FOUR

GOING BEYOND THE NEW DEAL—TRUMAN GETS A LIBERAL PLATFORM

ALTHOUGH THE DEMOCRATIC PARTY was more divided and disorderly than it had been for twenty years, the opening sentences in the 1948 platform were stirring and strong. There were no signs of defeatism or despair in any of its provisions. It was a platform aimed at rallying all the groups which had enabled Franklin Roosevelt to triumph in four elections.

The first statement in it expressed the conviction that "the destiny of the United States is to provide leadership in the world toward a realization of the Four Freedoms." The second sentence declared: "We chart our future course as we charted our course under the leadership of Franklin D Roosevelt and Harry S. Truman in the abiding belief that democracy—when dedicated to the service of all and not to a privileged few—proves its superiority over all other forms of government...."

The Four Freedoms were the primary points in President Roosevelt's address to Congress in January of 1941. He asserted that the nation stood for four basic freedoms vital for human progress: freedom of speech and expression; freedom of worship; freedom from want, by securing to every nation a healthy, peaceful life for its inhabitants; and freedom from fear, by reducing military arms everywhere. That global vision had encouraged and sustained millions of Americans in battles against totalitarian powers in Europe and Asia in World War II.

The American people, who had seemed to be demoralized and downhearted in the terrible depression of the 1930s, had astounded the world by their productive capacity and their valor in overcoming the Nazis, the Fascists and the Japanese militarists. It seemed reasonable to me and to many others in 1948 to proclaim that the United States could help every nation to secure "a healthy, peaceful life for its inhabitants" and could reduce arms everywhere on earth.

The other powerful nations on the planet—including the victors as well as the losers in the world war—had suffered staggering losses during the six years of carnage from 1939 to 1945. Only the United States had emerged from the struggle with a booming economy and huge resources of all kinds. There seemed to be no limits to what Americans could achieve. So I was delighted by the self-congratulatory statements approved by the Platform Committee:

"Ours is the party which rebuilt a shattered economy, rescued our banking system, revived our agriculture, re-invigorated our industry, gave labor strength and security, and led the American people to the broadest prosperity in our history.

"Ours is the party which introduced the spirit of humanity into our law, as we outlawed child labor and the sweatshop, insured bank deposits, protected millions of homeowners and farmers from foreclosure, and established national social security.

"Ours is the party under which this nation before Pearl Harbor gave aid and strength to those countries which were holding back the Nazi and Fascist tide.

"Ours is the party which stood at the helm and led the nation to victory in the war. Ours is the party which, during the war, prepared for peace so well that when peace came reconversion promptly led to the greatest production and employment in this nation's life...."

Those statements were boastful. We Democrats were thumping our chests and patting ourselves on the backs. Yet I had lived through the Depression and the war years that followed—and my personal experience convinced me those statements were true. I thought it fair for us Democrats to claim the credit we deserved. The Republicans had claimed credit for the prosperity of the 1920s—and had held the White House for twelve years because many voters had accepted their claims.

The Republicans under Herbert Hoover had been unable to cope with the economic collapse that occurred after the stock market crashed. Millions of men and women had lost their jobs—including my father.

Then Roosevelt had pushed through a series of federal laws that helped many people, including the Works Progress Administration and the Home Owners Loan Corporation, which enabled my family and many other families to survive. My parents were able to keep their house in Kansas City, although the family had to move temporarily to Indianapolis when my father was employed by the Veterans Administration.

Before the New Deal, many children were forced to work long hours for low wages. I was one of them. For a few months I labored twelve hours a days for 25 cents an hour in a box factory in Indianapolis. My family needed the income I brought home, but I lived on the edge of exhaustion. Then I sold a story called "The Light Bender" to *Wonder Stories*, a science fiction magazine, and I escaped from that sweat shop. But I remembered the grinding pain of the young people who had to work under those conditions.

In the dark years of the depression I produced a series of stories about future explorations and voyages to other planets. My hopes for the future were lifted by the transformation of the United States from a nation with millions of unemployed and hungry people to a nation with amazing opportunities available to people from a wide variety of backgrounds. That transformation had been accomplished by the liberal Democrats. So I was proud to be in Philadelphia, hailing the magnificent strides our country had made in fifteen years. I was glad the platform-drafters believed the United States could lead the way to a global community in which all nations would be at peace and would have everything needed for an abundant life. I believed the United Nations could be developed into such a community if the United States gave it enough support.

The 1948 platform declared: "We support the United Nations fully and we pledge our wholehearted aid toward its growth and development.... We will continue our efforts toward the establishment of an international armed force to aid its authority.... We advocate the grant of a loan to the UN—recommended by the President, but denied by the Republican Congress—for the construction of the United Nations headquarters in this country...." I was especially pleased by that last statement. I thought it was extremely important to have the UN's offices located in the United States, as a symbol of our commitment to its existence and its flourishing. I knew that Truman had been personally interested in the idea of a world parliament for many years. Joseph Guilfoyle, who had been on Truman's senatorial staff, had told me he had been asked by Truman to do research in the Library of Congress on methods of forming a global institution. Guilfoyle also mentioned to me Truman carried in his wallet a poem by Alfred Tennyson predicting the eventual creation of such a parliament. In that poem—entitled *Locksley Hall*, written in 1842—the English author wrote:

"For I dipt into the future, far as human eye could see,
Saw the Vision of the world, and all the wonder that could be;
Saw the heavens fill with commerce, argosies of magic sales,
Pilots of the purple twilight dropping down with costly bales;
Heard the heavens filled with shouting, and there rained a ghastly dew
From the nations' airy navies grappling in the central blue...
Till the war-drum throbb'd no longer, and the battle flags were furl'd
In the Parliament of Man, the Federation of the World...."

I was amazed by Tennyson's depiction of aerial warfare in a poem composed in 1842, but I knew that other visionary writers had made similar predictions. I, too, had gazed into the future. In my science fiction stories—such as "The Light Bender" and "Red April, 1965"—I had described wars in which long-range rockets were used. Then I had written about the development of a planetary organization and a time of enduring peace for humanity.

Despite the outbreaks of violence in many places, in spite of the atrocities committed by ethnic groups against one another, I felt that human beings would eventually decide that war had to be abolished. So I favored these statements which appeared in the Democratic platform: "We advocate the effective international control of weapons of mass destruction, including the atomic bomb, and we approve continued and vigorous efforts within the United Nations to bring about the successful consummation of the proposals which our government has advanced...." If President Truman's plan for international jurisdiction over atomic weapons had been adopted, the nuclear arms race would not have occurred—and humanity would not have been brought to the brink of annihilation in later confrontations between the United States and the Soviet Union.

Another important plank in the platform endorsed Truman's rapid recognition of the new State of Israel. Over the opposition of high officials in his administration—including Secretary of State George Marshall—Truman had recognized Israel immediately after its formation and he had helped the new Jewish nation to survive during the bloody conflicts in Palestine.

The platform affirmed his actions: "President Truman... led the world in extending friendship and welcome to a people who have long sought and justly deserve freedom and independence." No mention was made then of the Arab residents of Palestine, who fiercely opposed the establishment of Israel in what they considered to be their homeland. The writers of the platform pledged "appropriate aid to the State of Israel in developing its economy and resources...."

Although some of the consequences of his decision to support Israel were painful, Truman felt he had to do what he did. He was accused of acting emotionally—succumbing to the pleas of Eddie Jacobson, his former partner in a clothing store, and other Jewish friends—or of pandering to the wealthy Jews who gave many financial contributions to the Democratic Party.

Truman was certainly aware of the political significance of his decision, but it seemed clear to me—and to others who talked with him about his action—that his primary motivation came from his reading of the Bible. He believed that the Jewish people should have a homeland in the Middle East. He was one of the few American leaders who had tried strenuously to save the Jews of Europe from Hitler's concentration camps.

In April 1943, after he learned Jews had been "herded like animals" into those camps, he voiced his indignation in a vehement speech to 125,000 persons in a Chicago stadium. Saying that "no one can any longer doubt the horrible intentions of the Nazi beasts," Truman urged all the governments at war with the Nazis to help the Jews before it was too late. He asked for the opening of "free lands" for the Jews and other persecuted minorities.

"We know that they plan the systematic slaughter throughout all of Europe, not only of the Jews but of vast numbers of other innocent peoples," Truman said. "Today—not tomorrow—we must do all that is humanly possible to provide a haven and a place of safety for all those who can be grasped from the hands of the Nazi butchers."

Truman called upon all Americans to do more than make protests against Hitler's evil regime. He begged his fellow citizens to "draw deeply on our traditions of aid to the oppressed, and on our great national generosity." He said "This is not a Jewish problem, it is an American problem—and we must and we will face it squarely and honorably."

Unfortunately, the United States and other Allied governments did not respond to Truman's plea for the opening of "free lands" to the Jews and other persecuted people. Some Jews and other endangered persons were aided to escape from Hitler's Germany by President Roosevelt and other political and religious leaders. But Roosevelt was preoccupied with winning the war against the Nazis and the Japanese, and he did not confront the full horror of what was occurring the death camps. Israel came into existence finally because the Jews themselves acted to create a new nation—and Truman helped them at a crucial moment.

The Democratic platform in 1948 did not, of course, acknowledge the failures of the Roosevelt administration or the unwillingness of many Americans to take in millions of refugees during the war and in the postwar years. I was one of the many citizens who had little awareness of the Nazi slaughter centers. I don't remember reading anything about Truman's impassioned speech of 1943. I was in the army then and was primarily concerned with my own survival.

The inability of people in many countries to face the monstrous behavior of the Nazis—and the general silence in the Western countries while millions of human beings were tortured and murdered—was one of the terrible scandals of this century. When I learned about Truman's effort to rescue "all those who can be grasped from the hands of the Nazi butchers" I felt a sorrow for humanity's failure—and my own failure to try to arouse my government to act before it was too late.

After Truman made his anguished decision to use atom bombs against Japan, some of his critics depicted him as a callous man who cared nothing about the lives of the people who died in those bombings. But he did care about them, just as he cared for the Jews and others who were exterminated in the Nazi camps. He reached heights of ethical concern which were probably beyond the reach of most men in his generation.

Truman hoped the Jews and Arabs could live peacefully together in Palestine. But more than a million Palestinians became refugees during the fighting between Arab and Jewish forces when Israel came into existence. Their plight did not produce humanitarian responses on an adequate scale from the Arab nations or from other countries. The responsibility of caring for them was placed upon the United Nations—with substantial support from the Truman administration.

The 1948 platform did not attempt to indicate a policy of establishing a stable situation for the Palestinians as well as the Jews in the Middle East. In that election year, the focus of attention was on the Jews. Arabs did not have a powerful influence in American life. Republicans as well as Democrats supported the formation of Israel—and leaders in both parties eagerly sought contributions from Jewish citizens.

The platform did contain a pledge to sponsor "legislation to admit a minimum of 40,000 displaced persons found eligible for United States citizenship without discrimination as to race or religion." I favored that pledge, feeling that it might give new opportunities for thousands of Palestinians as well as Jews and others. I knew that many of the refugees were talented and highly motivated people who would be valuable citizens. I had advocated the admission of 1 million persons, but the platform committee members did not think that the Democratic convention would go for such a huge number.

In a message to Congress in 1945, Truman had called for an "economic bill of rights" including "the right to adequate medical care" and the right to have "adequate protection against the economic effects of sickness." He asserted that "everyone should have ready access to all necessary medical, hospital, and related services." He thought the costs could be met by "a system of required prepayments."

Truman had been disturbed in Word War II when Selective Service medical examinations revealed what he called "the widespread physical and mental incapacity among the young people of our nation." Reporting those conditions to the Congress, he stated: "We should resolve now that the health of this nation is a national concern; that the health of all its citizens deserves the help of all the nation." He insisted he was not advocating "socialized medicine" but seeking the creation of a national insurance system available to all.

To Truman's regret, the party platform did not endorse his comprehensive recommendations. These sentences appeared: "We favor the enactment of a national health program for expanded medical research, medical education, and hospitals and clinics. We will continue our efforts to aid the blind and other handicapped persons to become self-supporting We will continue... to expand maternal care, improve the health of the nation's children, and reduce juvenile delinquency...." Those statements, while they were generally progressive, did not go nearly as far as Truman wanted to go.

The platform, however, contained many other provisions based on Truman's fundamental conviction that the federal government should attempt to respond to all the needs of the people. In addition to a call for consideration of an equal rights amendment for women, the extension of voting rights to citizens in the District of Columbia, and the establishment of a National Science Foundation, the platform endorsed efforts to conserve natural resources for future generations, the extension of social security benefits to "all workers not now covered," and federal aid to education "administered by and under the control of the states."

As I worked on that platform in consultation with the other members of the Research Division and the White House staff, I became increasingly impressed by Truman's willingness to go beyond Roosevelt's New Deal. I began to see that Truman might be a bolder leader in some respects than Roosevelt had been.

In one field, some of the young leaders in the party successfully challenged Truman and defeated him—with explosive results, which threatened to disrupt his whole campaign. That was in the battle over civil rights.

The drafters of the platform struggled to bridge the cleavages in the party on what should be done about advancing the rights of black people and other minorities. Truman had supported the Fair Employment Practices committee established by Roosevelt in 1941; he had desegregated the armed forces; and he had created a Committee on Civil Rights by an executive order in 1946, asserting that "we are making progress, but we are not making progress fast enough." Believing that his record was clear, he sought to avoid a direct clash at the convention with Southern delegates.

But Hubert Humphrey—who was then the mayor of Minneapolis and a leader of the Minnesota delegation—had other ideas. Humphrey was one of the leaders who felt that Supreme Court Justice William Douglas would make a better presidential candidate than Truman in 1948. When the platform was presented to the national convention, Humphrey and other delegates offered a statement on civil rights that brought on a fight with the Southern leaders who believed that "the rights of the states" had to be protected.

I was in the hall when Humphrey stepped to the podium. He had a fresh, bright face, shining with perspiration. He was just 36 years old—much younger than the other leaders there. But what Humphrey said that day changed the atmosphere in the convention and produced repercussions for decades: "There are those who say to you—we are rushing this issue of civil rights," Humphrey shouted to the delegates. "I say we are 172 years late.... The time has come for the Democratic Party to get out of the shadow of states' rights and walk forthrightly into the bright sunshine of human rights."

In his declaration that "we are 172 years late" Humphrey referred to the Declaration of Independence, adopted in 1776. That Declaration had proclaimed that "all men are created equal"—and Thomas Jefferson, its principal author, had wanted it to apply to every citizen of the United States. But the institution of slavery had become established in the Southern states and the rights envisioned in the Declaration were not extended to all people for many decades.

There was a tremendous response to Humphrey's eloquence. Dozens of delegates from two states—California and Illinois—charged into the aisles. Hundreds of others followed, while a large band led by a union leader provided loud music. I found myself cheering, although I was afraid that the plank advocated by Humphrey and members of the liberal Americans for Democratic Action would make it impossible for Truman to carry all the states he needed for a victory in November.

Actually, the statement offered by Humphrey and his supporters specifically commended President Truman for "his courageous stand on the issue of civil rights." The statement called upon the Congress to back the President by guaranteeing four basic rights. "(1) the right of full and equal political participation; (2) the right to equal opportunity of employment; (3) the right of security of person; and (4) the right of equal treatment in the service and defense of our nation." A majority of the delegates recognized that the time had come to recognize those rights for all.

Many black citizens had been kept from voting by poll-tax laws and other unjust measures; many of them had been barred from high-level jobs and professional positions; many had been personally injured by physical attacks; and black soldiers had been forced to serve in segregated units in World War II. If the United States was to live up to the principles of a truly democratic society, black people and other citizens had to be given the status to which they were entitled.

After the platform had been approved, the time finally came for the selection of candidates for president and vice president. The "states' rights" delegates, led by Strom Thurmond, had marched out of the hall. As leaders from state after state announced the results from their delegations, it became quickly evident that Harry Truman could not be turned aside. Justice Douglas had made it clear that he did not want to be a candidate, and the anti-Truman delegates could not unite behind any other man.

On the first roll-call, Truman received 947 votes—a resounding majority. Paul McNutt, a popular man from Indiana, got one-half of a vote. Senator Richard Russell of Georgia obtained 263 votes from Southern delegates who had refused to leave the hall with Thurmond and his followers.

When Truman's nomination was announced, I thought of what the man had been forced to endure. He had waited for hours just outside the hall while his fellow Democrats wrangled and wobbled. As an incumbent President, he had enormous resources at his disposal. During his four years in the White House he had made some of the most significant decisions in history. His actions had changed the world—and possibly the future of humanity.

Yet his political life had been at stake in that sweaty gathering of politicians in Philadelphia. What counted for those men and women was the number of votes he could get in the autumn election. Many of them admired his personal strength and courage. But they weren't sure he could draw the right people to the polls from Maine to California when the crunch came in November.

Senator Alben Barkley of Kentucky—who had expressed his willingness to go on the ticket after Douglas had rejected Truman's offer of the vice presidential nomination—was swiftly accepted by the delegates as Truman's running mate. While Barkley made a brief speech, many of the delegates fanned themselves under the banners of their states. Many of the men's shirts were open and their ties were hanging loose.

It wasn't a dignified way to choose the Democratic candidates for the highest offices in the land. It was a messy process. A mayor from Minneapolis had gathered enough delegates to compel a president to accept a civil rights declaration which had split the Party. The president hadn't been able to get the man he wanted for his running mate.

The people in the hall showed no signs of waiting eagerly for the appearance of Harry Truman. I sat on the edge of my chair, because I hoped Truman would deliver his acceptance speech with enough fire and eloquence to arouse them. I had offered some suggestions for that speech, but I didn't know whether he would use any of them.

It was almost 2 o'clock in the morning when the President came striding to the podium. I wasn't prepared for what happened then. I was suddenly lifted by a wave of exultation—and that wave swept through the ranks of the men and women there, erasing their weariness, putting pride and joy on their faces.

Truman triumphed!

CHAPTER FIVE

*TRUMAN'S TRANSFORMATION—HE RISES HIGH
AND LIFTS HIS PARTY WITH HIM*

WHEN HARRY TRUMAN stepped to the microphones in that steaming hall, he was greeted by a flight of white birds. Flocks of doves and pigeons were released into the air to symbolize the Party's commitment to peace. The dazed birds flew in all directions, hitting the spotlights, fluttering toward the balcony, showering their droppings on spectators and delegates.

Standing on the podium in a spotless white suit, Truman didn't permit the circling birds to bother him for a moment. His voice crackled with fire through the loudspeakers. His first sentences conveyed his passion and his confidence. "Senator Barkley and I will win this election and make those Republicans like it," he snapped. "Don't you forget that."

If I hadn't been in that hall, I wouldn't have believed what I saw then. The half-dead delegates jumped to their feet. They waved their arms toward the man in the white suit. They began to whoop and yell.

Dismissing all the battles within the Party, Truman shouted: "It is time for us to get together and beat the common enemy. We will do that because they are wrong and we are right." Those were the words the delegates had been longing to hear. Truman didn't have the aristocratic presence of Franklin Roosevelt or the rolling oratory of a Winston Churchill, but he spoke with the authority of a prophet that night. He assured the delegates that they were taking part in something wonderful, something exciting—a noble struggle, not for themselves but for all the people whose lives had become more abundant in the Democratic years.

Those tired men and women were lifted up by the radiant presence of a man who had an elemental strength—a man who had been scorned and abandoned by many of the bigwigs in his own party as well as by the newspaper pundits and radio commentators. He had received many blows but he refused to go down. He had the aura of a man who truly believed he was fighting for a righteous cause.

In my newspaper days I had been imbued with cynicism. The editors who taught me the journalistic trade were skeptical about every human action and every human claim. I had been exhorted to remember that every man was flawed—and nobody could be fully trusted. As a reporter watching the behavior of people brought into police headquarters in Kansas City—and the behavior of the cops—I saw scenes that disgusted me.

But I saluted Harry Truman on that tumultuous night in Philadelphia. I could understand why the men in his artillery unit were so loyal to him in war and peace. He had all the qualities of a democratic leader. He respected them and they reciprocated.

In that crowd of stomping, shouting delegates I felt a hope for humanity—a hope which had burned in me as a soldier in England on D Day—June 6, 1944—when I heard the voice of General Dwight D. Eisenhower announcing that the liberation of Western Europe had begun. Allied troops were landing on the beaches of France—spilling their blood to end the savage reign of Adolf Hitler. I landed in Normandy later, and went on to take part in the liberation of Paris. I had done very little, but I was given a full share of the ecstasy of the golden day when we entered the capital of France. I knew that thousands of men had died to drive the Germans back, but I welcomed the embraces and the kisses of those who greeted us when we came into the beautiful city.

Once again—on that night when Truman summoned all of us to fight the forces of evil—I shared in a time of jubilation far greater than I had ever expected. As he spoke, I noted that he had used much of the material we had gathered for him in the Research Division but he used it in a way that was far more effective than I had anticipated.

Truman called for a crusade—a crusade for the rights and liberties of the people, a crusade against the Republican plutocrats and the corporate lobbyists who had defeated his proposals in the 80th Congress. He urged the voters to realize that their prosperity was at stake in the

1948 election. "The total national income has increased from less than 40 billion dollars in 1933 to 203 billion dollars in 1947—the greatest in the history of the world," Truman said. "These benefits have been spread to all the people, because it is the business of the Democratic Party to see that the people get a fair share of these things."

I knew the benefits had been spread unevenly during those years—with the people in the upper brackets getting more than the poor—but the President's figures were generally accurate. He did not emphasize the economic effects of World War II, when the United States had put millions of people to work in the gigantic production programs necessary to overcome Germany and Japan. Many of the war workers earned better wages than they had ever attained before. The programs had been conducted on a bipartisan basis, but it was true that the country had leaped to unprecedented heights in the fourteen years Truman cited.

If Hitler had not risen to power in Germany and if the Japanese militarists had not attempted to create a vast empire—compelling the United States to meet those challenges—the income of the people might have grown much more slowly. Yet, it could not be denied that Americans had responded to those threats with magnificent productivity under the leadership of Roosevelt and Truman.

Truman briefly acknowledged the essential support given to the Marshall Plan and other programs by Republican leaders. He said the country had been "turned away permanently from isolationism," and added, "We have converted the greatest and best of the Republicans to our viewpoint on that subject."

"The United States has to accept its full responsibility for leadership in international affairs," Truman said, thrusting his jaw forward. "We have been the backers and the people who organized and started the United Nations—first started under that great Democratic president, Woodrow Wilson, as the League of Nations. The League was sabotaged by the Republicans in 1920. We must see that the United Nations continues a strong and growing body, so we can have everlasting peace in the world."

While I shared Truman's view that the League had been wrecked by partisanship in the United States Senate, I thought he was wrong in asserting that the fate of the United Nations depended almost entirely on the Democratic Party. I shuddered when I heard Truman strike such a heavy blow at the Republicans; I thought he should have emphasized the necessity for bipartisan support of the UN. The survival of the UN might depend on Republicans as well as Democrats.

Claiming more credit for himself and his fellow Democrats, Truman continued, "We removed trade barriers in the world, which is the best asset we can have for peace.... We have started the foreign aid program, which means the recovery of Europe and China and the Far East. We instituted the program for Greece and Turkey...." He did not mention the reconstruction of Japan, which had been carried out by General Douglas MacArthur under Truman's authorization. The Japanese government had been transformed into a democracy, with power transferred from the Emperor to a popularly elected House of Representatives. A tremendous economic recovery was under way in Japan—with repercussions around the world.

After his review of the accomplishments he had cited, Truman abruptly admitted, "I will say to you that all these things were done in a cooperative and bipartisan manner. The Foreign Relations Committees of the Senate and the House were taken into the full confidence of the President in every one of these moves, and don't let anybody tell you anything else. As I have said time and time again, foreign policy should be the policy of the whole nation and not the policy of one party or the other. Partisanship should stop at the water's edge...."

Truman had certainly consulted the leading Republicans in the House and the Senate. Arthur Vandenberg, the chairman of the Senate Foreign Relations Committee, had played a key role persuading the Congress to pass the Marshall Plan and to support the Truman Doctrine of providing aid to countries threatened by communism. As President, Truman had acknowledged Vandenberg's role. As a party leader in Philadelphia, Truman did not do it.

In the heat of a campaign, it was almost impossible for a candidate to maintain the lofty tone of a statesman. As President, Truman was well aware of the necessity for transcending partisan limitations. In the convention hall on that hot night in July, he knew the delegates expected him to roast the Republicans—and that he did.

Like the delegates around me, I encouraged Truman to hit harder and harder. We were on the side of truth and goodness, and we were sure that the Republicans were dominated by the forces of evil. We yelled when Truman said: "Ever since its inception, that party has been under the control of special privilege, and they have completely proved it in the 80th Congress. They proved it in the things they did to the people, and not for them. They proved it by the things they failed to do."

I shared Truman's rage against that Congress. Many members had been submissive to the lobbyists for corporations and for rich people seeking favors. That Congress had failed to act on programs designed to clear away the slums in the big cities and stimulate the building of low-cost housing across the nation. That Congress had approved the Taft-Hartley Act, which disrupted labor-management relations and caused strife between employees and employers. It had refused to fund the building of schools needed in many states. It took away social security benefits from 750,000 persons. It blocked consideration of Truman's civil rights bills and killed his proposal for a national health care system. But I was uneasy when Truman said that the Republican Party had been "under the control of special privilege" from its beginning. The party had nominated and elected Abraham Lincoln, and many of its members had upheld Lincoln in his struggle to save the Union and emancipate the slaves. It generally represented "business interests" but liberal leaders had occasionally achieved power in it. Theodore Roosevelt, a Republican President, had fought for the preservation of natural resources and made attempts to regulate the giant corporate "trusts' and had assailed "the malefactors of great wealth."

Harry Truman knew all that history, of course, but he did not let it deter him from excoriating the Republican legislators who had captured the Congress in 1946. He was firmly convinced that it would be disastrous for the people to permit those Republicans to retain their control of Congress and to elect a President who might undo the social reforms of the New Deal. And I thought he was right about that.

I did not acknowledge to myself then—or for several years after that night of partisan enthusiasm—that many conservative Democrats were as reactionary as the Republicans. I tried to believe that Truman had really gained the support of a majority of those who called themselves Democrats. I had committed myself to Truman's flag—and I hoped millions of Americans would join his crusade.

As Truman delivered his acceptance speech, I waited for him to make the announcement all of us in the Research Division had recommended—the calling of a special session of Congress. I had a deep feeling such an action might be the essential step for his election.

I jumped and yelled when I heard him say, "On the 26th day of July—which out in Missouri we call 'Turnip Day'—I am going to call Congress back and ask them to pass laws to halt rising prices, to meet the housing crisis—which they are saying they are for in their platform…." Truman went on, "At the same time, I shall ask them to act upon other vitally needed measures, such as aid to education, which they say that are for; a national health program; civil rights legislation, which they say they are for; an increase in the minimum wage, which I doubt very much they are for; extension of the Social Security coverage and increased benefits, which they say they are for; funds for projects needed in our program to provide public power and cheap electricity…. I shall ask for adequate and decent laws for displaced persons in place of this anti-Semitic, anti-Catholic law which this 80th Congress passed…."

Truman referred to the "long list of promises" contained in the platform adopted by the Republicans in their convention a few weeks earlier. Then he commented, "Now, my friends, if there is any reality behind that Republican platform, we ought to get some action from a short session of the 80th Congress. They can do this job in 15 days, if they want to do it. They will still have time to go out and run for office."

When I returned to Washington after the Democratic convention ended, I threw myself into the campaign with a fervor that surprised my friends. I had seen Harry Truman in a new light. I was positive that the future of our country—and perhaps the fate of the earth—depended upon his continuance as President.

His closing words referred to the struggle in 1932. He declared: "In 1932 we were attacking the citadel of special privilege and greed. We were fighting to drive the money changers from the temple.... The battle cry is just the same now as it was in 1932.... My friends, with the help of God and the whole-hearted push which you can put behind this campaign, we can save this country...."

I remembered 1932. I feared a Republican president might bring back the terrible conditions that existed then. I remembered the despair I had seen in the faces of my father's friends—men who had lost their jobs and couldn't find openings anywhere. Some of them lost their homes and became alcoholics or committed suicide. I remembered the unemployed veterans who sold apples on the streets, and the men and women who lived in shacks made of cardboard and old boxes.

I knew the Founding Fathers of the United States had deplored partisanship and the first president, George Washington, had warned against it in his Farewell Address, but Washington had reluctantly decided that parties could not be ignored. Washington had tried to rise above what he called "the common and continued mischiefs of the spirit of Party," but he recognized the fact that he had to be a party leader in order to be an effective president.

In using his presidential power to get the Congress to reassemble in Washington, Truman declared that he was acting for "the general welfare"—for the best interests of the American people as a whole. He cited the points on which the Republicans had taken positions similar to those of the Democrats—and he regarded the special session as a test of their sincerity.

When the Senators and Representatives came back to the Capitol on July 26, angry debates began almost at once. In the Research Division, we had prepared speeches for leading Democrats in the Senate. We slammed the Republicans with all the facts and figures we could put together. We were eager to give a bad Congress "hell"—just as Harry Truman had done in Philadelphia. We didn't expect the Republicans to accomplish anything, and we found joy in reminding them of their failures to do what the president had asked them to do.

I was asked to write a scornful speech to be delivered by Senator Lucas, ridiculing the claims made by lobbyists for the National Association of Manufacturers and Republicans in Congress, who asserted that the abolition of price controls would bring lower prices through the operation of the "free market." Prices had skyrocketed after the controls had been removed. I produced a speech which impressed Lucas and Al Vigderman, who had returned to the Senator's staff.

Through Vigderman I learned the conservatives in the Senate were prepared to block Truman's program unless he won by a landslide. The special session exacerbated relations between the various factions in the Congress. It had repercussions that no one had anticipated—and I wondered how Truman would ever get the majorities he needed in the Senate and the House. Many voters in many parts of the country might favor Truman's liberal measures, but the entrenched members of Congress in both parties could ignore their views.

As a journalist, I had been skeptical about the desire of the politicians to serve the public. Truman had convinced me that he was genuinely motivated by such a desire. But the more I admired the President, the more clearly I saw that he would probably be blocked and frustrated—just as Franklin Roosevelt had often been stymied after the first years of the New Deal. If Truman had been more diplomatic in his treatment of his opponents—if he had attributed good motives even to the Republicans he denounced—would the country have been better served? Looking back from the perspectives I have gained through the years, I see now that the 1948 campaign inflicted deep wounds on everyone who participated in it. It inflamed the political atmosphere of the 1950s and had negative effects in the subsequent decades.

Could Truman have taken a different road? If he had simply emphasized his achievements during his years in the White House—and had refrained from labeling Republican leaders as "the enemy"—would he have carried as many states as he did? Given his feeling that he had been unfairly attacked, given his belief in the rightness of his program and the wrongness of the opposition, would it have been possible for him to have campaigned in a different style?

David Lloyd, who moved from the Research Division to the White House staff, told me he had been with Truman one evening when a recording of one of the President's speeches was played. "What demagoguery!" Truman exclaimed, when he heard himself delivering a partisan line. "Why did I say that?" And then the President chuckled, "Demagoguery—that's part of the game."

Certainly the other candidates in that year engaged in demagoguery—appealing to the passions and prejudices of the people. Many presidential campaigns—and other political struggles in the country's history—had been marred by wild charges and counter-charges. Perhaps the American people expected their candidates to be dramatic performers, entertaining and arousing the voters by every possible means.

In going through my life, in searching through all my experiences, in trying to see the events of my time from a thousand viewpoints, in striving to escape from my own denials of my mistakes and failures, I think I have reached more understanding of how difficult it is for men in combat to treat their opponents with compassion. A man who feels that his cause is right—as Truman did—often is reluctant to concede any merit to those who are attacking him.

One night in October, as the campaign approached its end, I sat in a room in the White House with Truman, Mrs. Truman, their daughter Margaret, and a dozen staff members who were there to watch him make a radio broadcast to the nation. What happened that night indicated to me that Truman's manhood—his conception of himself as a masculine leader—was at stake in the political battle.

Mr. Truman was seated at a small desk on which a microphone had been placed. His wife and daughter sat close to him. The President beamed at all of us. He appeared to be completely relaxed. According to the latest polls, he was heading toward a humiliating defeat. Yet he looked as confident to me as he had when I had first seen him in Clifford's office in the spring.

A radio in one corner of the room made a crackling sound, and everyone leaned forward. We heard an announcer say: "Miss Tallulah

71

Bankhead, speaking from New York, will introduce President Truman tonight." Miss Bankhead was in her dressing room in a Broadway theater. She spoke from there.

In her day—long before the rise of Marilyn Monroe and other Hollywood goddesses—Tallulah Bankhead of Alabama was an actress who stirred the emotions of many men. She was a daughter of William Bankhead, who had been a Democratic Speaker of the House of Representatives and she was exceptionally free in her speech and actions. "I want you to vote for Harry Truman because he is a *true* man," Miss Bankhead said in her throaty, deeply sensual voice. She convinced everybody that she knew what a "true man" was—and that a true woman admired a genuinely masculine man.

The President ducked his head and spoke to us in a quick aside, "She's implying that Tom Dewey is not a real man. I don't like that." But he was grinning broadly. He went on the air with crisp vigor in his voice—the vigor of a full-blooded, healthy man.

It seemed to me that Tallulah's description of him was exactly right. He had the masculine qualities Americans admired. He had proved his bravery in war and peace. He was true to his wife, true to his friends, true to his political party, true to his country. If those were the qualities voters were looking for, Truman might be given four more years in the White House.

Truman delivered his radio broadcast in the short sentences he liked. After he had finished, he invited our comments—reminding us that he wanted us to speak plainly. If we had suggestions for improving his delivery or his talk, he was ready to hear them. Nobody offered any criticisms. In every speech, he seemed to get more impressive.

When the President, Mrs. Truman and Margaret left the radio room I went with the staff members into the corridor behind them. As they walked away I found myself in step with Jonathan Daniels, a North Carolina newspaperman who had been on Franklin Roosevelt's staff. Unlike some of the other men in the Roosevelt administration who had deserted Truman, Daniels was doing everything he could to rally support for Truman.

"He's getting better all the time," Daniels said. "He'll never be another Roosevelt, but he is surprising a lot of people." I replied, "I'm beginning to think that he'll win." Daniels gripped my arm. "Don't get your hopes up too far, Frank. At this stage of a campaign, people close to the candidate develop a euphoria. Don't let it carry you away. If you completely identify with him, you'll be torn apart when he loses."

"When he loses?" I said, feeling a cold weight in my stomach. "He may be gaining but he has a long way to go," Daniels said, as we came to the end of the corridor. "Keep your cool. You've got plenty of possibilities ahead of you, whatever happens."

I didn't know whether Daniels was aware of my appointment to the faculty at Boston University. Walter Winchell, the gossip columnist, had printed an item saying: "Frank Kelly, one of Truman's speech writers, has given up on Truman's campaign and has lined up a job at Boston University, starting in November...." I had asked Charlie Murphy to explain to the President why I had agreed to that appointment. Murphy had informed me that Truman understood that I was primarily a writer and a journalist, not seeking a political career.

As I left the White House that night, I shared Daniels' opinion that there were "plenty of possibilities" ahead for me. The Atlantic Monthly Press editors wanted me to do a series of books. A professorship in Boston would be a challenging position. I would keep in touch with the Nieman Fellows at Harvard and I could take part in the lively intellectual life of the Boston-Cambridge community. It might not be as exciting as New York or Washington, but it would be eminently worthwhile.

In the closing weeks of the campaign Truman went from state to state, talking with people from early in the morning until late at night. Members of his staff who traveled on the train came back to Washington exhausted, but they told us that the President seemed tireless. He was exhilarated by the cordiality and applause of the people he encountered. He was sure that they understood why he had turned to them—and he was confident that the results in November would stun the pundits.

When I learned the President was going to make a major speech in Boston on October 27, I told Bill Batt I had been invited to be in the city on the 26th for a meeting at Boston University, and expressed a desire to be with the Truman group in Boston. I was eager to be near the President when he spoke in New England, wanting to see how the crowds reacted to him. I was tired of sitting in an office, pouring out words for his use.

So, I went to Boston with a White House card given to me by George Elsey, which cleared the way for me to reach Truman's hotel suite. As I approached the open door, I heard the sound of a piano. The President was relaxing—playing one of his favorite waltzes. Listening to that music, I realized again that Harry Truman was a gifted man in fields beyond politics. He had a sensitive appreciation of poetry and music. He was able to put aside his campaigning to enjoy the arts.

As I entered the suite, the President ended the waltz with a flourish and a wide smile. "Let's go, boys," he said. "We can't keep a crowd of good Democrats waiting. It won't be long now before we are finished with all this traveling."

I encountered Wallace Graham, the President's physician. As we moved toward the hotel lobby, Dr. Graham invited me to ride with him to the hall where Truman was scheduled to speak. I thanked him for that opportunity.

The lobby was packed with yelling people. Many of them were waving and clapping. Policemen and Secret Service agents cleared a narrow path for the President to walk to the automobile that was waiting for him. Dr. Graham took my arm and pulled me along through those lines of men and women. I heard shouts: "Keep it up, Harry!" "We're with you!" "You're going to win, Harry!" Truman beamed and smiled, turning his head from side to side, shaking as many hands as he could reach.

"It has been like this all day," Dr. Graham muttered. "We've never seen such crowds. They're wild about him." He and I got into an open car, just behind the one in which the President was riding. I knew why Truman's physician had to be close to him. If any shots were fired, if Truman suffered any injury, his doctor had to be near.

I remembered when an assassin had tried to kill Franklin Roosevelt. Other Presidents had been murdered. But that night I didn't feel any sense of danger. I was carried along by a great wave of affection expressed by the people for Harry Truman. People voiced their love and their hopes for him as we moved through the streets of Boston.

Men and women called him "Harry" but their respect for him was palpable. He was their man in Washington. He was the President but he was connected to them on a personal basis. He was a man who went for brisk walks every morning—and mailed many of his own letters. He was a man who accepted the awesome powers and responsibilities of the presidential position, but he never lost sight of his own humanity.

I remembered when Truman had been a county judge in Kansas City. In the Jackson County Courthouse he had been a familiar figure— striding through the corridors, riding in the elevators. His rise to the White House had not been anticipated then by any of us in Kansas City or his home town of Independence. But he had shown his abilities to deal with the tremendous problems he had faced after he had been cat-apulted into the presidency.

That night in Boston stirred up in me another awareness of the tremendous adventure into which I had been pulled by an accident of friendship. I didn't know what might be in store for Harry Truman, or for me. I was simply grateful for the opportunities I had already received—and I looked forward to some astounding surprises.

CHAPTER SIX

AS THE CAMPAIGN CLOSES, TRUMAN DRAWS HUGE CROWDS AND VICTORY SEEMS POSSIBLE

As I RODE WITH DR. GRAHAM in the car behind Truman on that roaring night in October, savoring the tumultuous reception he received in Boston, I tried to imagine what it was like to be a President who had been downgraded and deserted in July—and then in the last weeks of his campaign acclaimed as a hero. Men and women were yelling and running, struggling to get close to him. I saw people saluting him from the windows of the buildings around us.

"I'm feeling again that he might win," I said, leaning toward Dr. Graham. "Up here, he has already won," Dr. Graham said. "He has reached the hearts of these people."

Our motorcade had to stop frequently while the police pushed and persuaded people to return to the sidewalks. In one of those pauses, I called out to a beefy officer sitting on a motorcycle near us. "How does this crowd compare with Roosevelt's?" I asked him. "Roosevelt never drew a crowd half this size," the policeman answered in an Irish accent. "I've been on the force twelve years and I've never seen a mob this big. We like Harry better than Roosevelt. He's a grand man."

When we reached the auditorium, I went over to the newspapermen who were getting out of cars behind us. "What do you make of this crowd?" I asked them. The men with the press badges shrugged. One of them said, "I guess a lot of people like Harry all right. That doesn't mean they're all going to vote for him."

As we entered the auditorium, the noise of the people packed in there was deafening. Some of them were waving flags and others were clapping. A band was playing a lively tune.

When the President was introduced, we heard the stately music of

76

"Hail to the Chief." He went to the microphones with the sound of power around him. He was more than "a grand man" at that moment. He represented the strength of the American Dream. He stood before them as their servant and their leader.

"There are some Republicans who have been trying to make you believe that your government is endangered by communist infiltration," Truman snapped. "That is a malicious falsehood." The crowd roared. People shouted, "Pour it on, Harry! Pour it on!"

Truman reminded them that Tom Dewey—who had been the Republican presidential candidate against Roosevelt in 1944—had accused Roosevelt of "soliciting the support of Communists." Dewey had asserted that the communists were "seizing control of the New Deal."

Knowing that many of the people in his audience were Roman Catholics, Truman went on, "All of this Republican talk about communism in 1944 and again this year is in the same pattern with their appeals to religious prejudice against Al Smith in 1928." The crowd rumbled with anger. Al Smith—a Catholic—had been the Democratic nominee in 1928 and had been defeated in a bitter campaign. "Get this straight," Truman said. "I hate communism. I deplore what it does to the dignity and freedom of the individual. I detest the godless creed it preaches. I have fought it at home. I have fought it abroad. I shall continue to fight it with all my strength. I shall never surrender." Many people in the audience jumped to their feet and shouted their approval.

"Just look at the facts," Truman said. "The Communist Party of the United States is today supporting a third-party candidate in an effort to defeat me... The communists don't want me to be President because this country, under a Democratic administration, has rallied the forces of all the democracies of the world to safeguard freedom and to save free people everywhere from communist slavery."

Aware of the anxiety generated by the possibility of a war, Truman quickly added: "Our goal is peace. It is our conviction that peace in this atomic age is an absolute necessity. But only a peace that is based on human rights and freedom will be a lasting peace."

Truman then spoke of the European Recovery Program, which had succeeded with financial aid supplied by the United States under his leadership, "Our aid has given Italy a new lease on freedom. Our aid has helped rally decisive popular support for the freely elected government of Italy. It has shown the Italian people that they can solve their economic problems under democracy." Turning to the situation in France, he said, "There, as throughout Europe, we are using our economic strength to raise the living standards of the people, and thus to avoid the danger of a fascist reaction or a communist tyranny. The communists hold that against me, too."

He reaffirmed the decision he had made to supply Berlin by air after the Soviets had imposed a blockade around the western section of the city, "We have taken the frank and firm position that communism must not spread its tentacles into the western zones. We shall not retreat. We shall feed Berlin, and the people of Germany will be given their chance to work out a decent life under a democratic government...." Pounding the podium, Truman declared, "The real threat of communism in this country lies in the danger of another major depression. The real threat lies in widespread unemployment and arrogant injustice, such as we had in 1932.... Reactionary Republican policies invited communism then...."

In that auditorium in Boston, surrounded by people who were stirred by Truman's fighting spirit, I wished that he had not felt compelled to talk so much about his battles against communism at home and abroad. In a way, the loyalty-security program he had initiated in the federal government indicated that he had been swayed by the fears generated by the House Un-American Activities Committee, the Hearst newspapers, and right-wing radio commentators like Walter Winchell. He had not descended to their level, but investigations conducted under that program had harmed people who had belonged to liberal groups or associated with socialists or communists.

During my years in New York I had met some professed Marxists who denounced injustices and advocated better living conditions for people at the bottom of the economic scale. Perhaps they had deceived me, but I thought that they were genuinely concerned about the plight of the poor—especially the blacks, the Puerto Ricans, the immigrants who were jammed into the slums of New York. I did not regard them as threats to the United States. I believed they were pursuing a dream of *equality,* which had always been one of the promises of American life.

In his speech in Boston—as well as in other speeches he made as the election came closer—he expressed his belief that the American people would defeat "the red menace of communism" just as they had helped to save "the free peoples of the world" from the "menace of fascism." He did not emphasize the role of the United Nations, although he was one of the founders of that world organization in 1945.

"You can fight communism with a clear-cut vote to defeat Republican reaction," Truman said. The Boston crowd responded with a roar.

When I left that hall that night, I had a feeling that Truman was evoking enough popular support to beat his three opponents. If he could get his supporters to go to the polls he could pull off an electoral upset that would stun the political experts.

The experience of being with the President on the campaign trail gave me a perception of the deep connection he had made with the people. His strong presence as a man with high leadership abilities had an electrifying effect upon many of the citizens who saw and heard him. The newsreels and the newspapers did not convey the full impact of Truman's passionate appeals.

During the years when he had been a near-sighted boy with thick glasses in Independence, reading all the books he could reach in the public library, Truman had become conscious of the power of words. He regarded poets as more important than generals or statesmen. He had been labeled by some reporters as a whiskey-drinking, poker-playing politician with a barnyard vocabulary, but he was a much more complicated man than they had begun to realize.

The music he had been playing in his hotel suite that evening meant more to him than the cheers he received during his journey from the hotel to the auditorium—or the roaring of the crowd in that cavernous place. The poem by Alfred Tennyson he had in his wallet was always accessible to him when he needed to remind himself that poets drew upon the mysterious powers of prophets. Through poetry the President soared from the past into a dazzling future.

That night in Boston led me to understand Truman's apparent sereni-ty, his buoyant manner, his dauntless spirit. I hoped that some day I could write about him with the inspiration of a poet. I didn't think that my life would be linked with his after the election. I didn't have any inkling that I would always be marked as a man who served under Truman's banner.

I thought my future would be shaped by the books I expected to write. The excitement of politics was enticing, but I didn't want to stay in it. There would never be another campaign as embracing as Truman's long struggle. I expected my life as a professor to be rewarding in a dif-ferent way.

Before I had joined the President's entourage that night, I had been to the offices of the Atlantic Monthly Press and received a copy of my first book. The joy of holding the volume in my hands was like the plea-sure I felt when I held my first child in my arms. The kicking, squalling baby was much more alive than the book, of course. Being a father was a more marvelous moment of creativity for a man than producing a book. The boy in my arms gave me a realization that I was carrying on a Celtic line—a line that stretched back into the mists of the forests from which my ancestors came and a line that might go forward through cen-turies to come. I had wanted a child; and Barbara had responded to that desire, and from our love for each other an amazing new being had arrived in the world.

No experience would be greater than that. But the solidity of a book in my hands gave me a sense of achievement in a different realm. The book had my name on it. The words on the pages had poured from my mind. It was unlike any other book ever published in the history of the planet. It was beautiful, it was magical, it was alive in its own way. It might live longer than I would—or my sons and grandsons would. I hoped, of course, that it would live forever.

If I hadn't written that book, I wouldn't have been asked to join Truman's staff. I wouldn't have taken part in the drafting of a platform for the Democratic Party. I wouldn't have witnessed the transformation of the delegates at the national convention in Philadelphia. I wouldn't have been invited to ride with the President through the cheering crowds in Boston. I felt I would never ride in a President's procession again. I was glad it had gone peacefully through the packed streets. I don't know what I would have done if someone had wounded the President and fired shots at the car in which I rode with Dr. Graham. The Secret Service men would have rushed Truman and his physician to a hospital. There would have been an uproar in the city—perhaps a panic if Truman had been severely injured.

There were people who despised Truman and people who hated him, but there had been no expressions of anger or antagonism directed at him that night. He rode a wave of admiration from his hotel to the auditorium. He seemed invincible that night—but he knew that he was vulnerable and so did all of his guards and staff members.

Truman left Boston the next day to speak in other cities and towns. He had just five days in which to swing as many votes as he could. He carried with him the undeniable evidence that people responded to his words—people were turning toward him, not away from him. Even the newspapermen could see that.

My time of participation in the campaign was over. I had a meeting with faculty members at Boston University, where I was assured that I would be welcomed there on November 3, the day after the election. Their cordiality made me feel that I would enjoy my association with them.

I returned to New York and rushed to my apartment in Patchin Place. I rapped on the door and when Barbara opened it I placed my book in her hands. It was dedicated to her and to our son, Terry. Her encouragement had given me the courage to write it.

"The first of ten volumes," I said. "Ten?" she said. "You'll write more than ten." She whirled around and showed the gleaming book to Terry. Then we danced around the coffee table, laughing together.

"You'll have to give a copy of this one to Truman," Barbara said. "He loves books. You know that." "I'm not sure he'll have this one," I said. "And he won't have time to read it until the votes are counted."

I decided I would send a copy to Charlie Ross, the President's press secretary. Ross would read it, because he was concerned about everything that referred to his old friend, Harry Truman. Ross would realize that I had tried to describe truthfully how Truman had handled the show-down with Stalin which had led to the withdrawal of Soviet troops from Iran.

"How do you feel about Truman now?" I asked Barbara. "He got a tremendous reception in Boston but the correspondents still don't think he can possibly win." "They're looking at it as a game," she said. "Who's going to win? Who's going to lose? It's more serious than that. It's about the future of our country, and the people know that. Who is the best man? You know the answer to that." "I can guess," I said. "Tallulah Bankhead called him a true man."

"She was right," Barbara said, hugging me. "I'm proud that you've worked for him, whatever happens. He's the man for that job. I believe the people will figure it out." "A lot of people aren't as smart as you are," I muttered. "Yes, they are. You'll see!" "The Republicans will spend tons of money in the last days," I said. "They want to bury him, after what he's been saying about them. He's been pretty rough." "They can't bury him!" Barbara's eyes flashed. "It's too late for them to pour dirt on him now."

Suddenly I remembered the motorcycle patrolman, the big man sitting on his machine next to Dr. Graham's car, ready to protect the President if he could. The patrolman had said, "Roosevelt never drew a crowd half this size. We like Harry up here. He's a grand man."

Would that be enough? Would millions of people vote for him because he was "a grand man"—a "true man" as Tallulah Bankhead had described him? Was that the essential quality people sought in a president—a sense of masculine strength?

After all the work that had been done—all the days and nights we had spent in gathering "facts" and developing ideas, all the writing and rewriting of his hundreds of speeches by his staff and the men who were with him on his train, all the efforts made by the Democratic National Committee and thousands of citizens who defended him and supported him—would it boil down to his traits as a masculine leader, a man with fundamental virtues, a man who never surrendered?

"I'll never forget riding with him through the streets of Boston," I said. "I shared in the exultation of the people on the sidewalks, the people waving from windows. I'll never forget the roar in the auditorium, the voices of the crowd when he came in there and the band played "'Hail to the Chief.'"

Barbara touched my face. "Your forehead is hot," she said. "You've got the political fever, Frank. You won't be able to put it behind you." "I don't have to put it behind me," I said. "I'll always remember it." Her face clouded. "I wish I could have been with you." "You were," I said. "You were with me all the time. I wouldn't have been in this adventure if you hadn't persuaded me that I had to do what I could for Captain Harry."

Every weekend I had rushed from Washington to New York, to be with her and to be with Terry. I tried to tell her as much as I could about what was happening in the campaign. She had been invited to come to the White House radio room on the night when Truman made a broadcast to the nation, sponsored by the International Ladies Garment Workers Union. But our bank account was low, and the trip would have been expensive. If she had brought Terry, she could have stayed with David and Charlotte Lloyd at their house in Virginia. Yet she decided that we couldn't afford that trip. We had less than a hundred dollars in the bank.

"Maybe I'll get to go to the White House some time," she said. "After the election. We'll probably be invited to the inauguration." While she was speaking, the telephone rang. Shelby Storck was on the phone, telling us that he was with some of Truman's supporters in Kansas City. They were prepared to make bets on the outcome of the election. Shelby and I had won $600 apiece by wagering that Franklin Roosevelt would win a third term in 1940.

"What's the inside word?" Storck asked. "We want to put a bundle on Harry. There's a lot of Dewey money around. What odds should we get?" I had to tell him what Bill Batt had told me when I had talked with him a day earlier. The surveys done for the Democratic Committee indicated that Truman would probably lose New York and Pennsylvania because of the votes Henry Wallace would get on the Progressive ticket in those two states. That would make it very hard for Truman to gain enough electoral votes to give him the necessary margin.

"Are those late reports?" Storck asked. "Harry is pulling ahead here in

Missouri." "Sure, he'll carry Missouri," I said. "But there are plenty of other states that look doubtful. I'm getting a wild feeling myself that he's going to make it, but I can't bet on it." "You bet on Roosevelt," Storck said.

"I was edgy about that, too, but I didn't think anybody could beat Roosevelt," I said. "And nobody did. But Harry has had an uphill road. If I had a big bank account, I might put some of it on Truman, but I can't afford to take the risk right now. Barbara and I are preparing to move to Boston, and we've got a stack of expenses."

"If Truman wins, you'll be going back to Washington," Storck said. "He hasn't offered me a job," I said. "I'm putting politics behind me. I'm going to start another book and I'm going to teach."

"Wait a minute," Storck muttered. I heard other voices in the background. then Storck said, "Some of us here are still going to take a chance on Harry. And I'll make a little bet with you that you won't be in Boston very long."

"I've been appointed as an associate professor at Boston University," I said. "That can be a lifetime job. And I'll have plenty of time to write. I'm planning to stay up there." Storck laughed. "If Truman wins, you'll change your mind. They'll want you in Washington." "I don't think so," I said. "But I hope you win plenty if you bet on Harry." "The Dewey people here are willing to bet their shirts," Storck said. "I won't turn down an opportunity to take them to the cleaners."

When our conversation ended I sat in silence for a few moments. I remembered the day in October, 1940, when Storck and I had placed our wagers on Roosevelt with a group of professional gamblers in Kansas City. The gamblers had faces like weasels and I had wondered whether we would get our winnings if Roosevelt defeated Wendell Willkie. But the gamblers had paid us in cash on the day after the November election. I had used the money I won then to move to New York.

"Storck is going to go for Truman," I said to Barbara. Shelby was her friend as well as mine. I had met Barbara at Storck's house in Kansas City. She smiled. "I thought he would," she said. Then she took me in her arms and kissed me. "I wish we could bet everything we have in the . bank on Harry. He's going to surprise everybody." "Except you and Mary

Abbott," I said. I returned her kiss and rose to my feet. "We barely have enough money to get to Boston. We can't afford to do any gambling."

I had an impulse to call Storck and ask him whether I could borrow five hundred dollars. I didn't do it. I knew that he seldom had much money in his own bank account. "Maybe I could borrow a little from Mrs. Abbott," I said. "She thinks my book is going to sell pretty well. She knows that we would pay her back." Barbara shook her head. "We can't do that. I don't believe that she approves of gambling."

I remembered the day when I had been told that MGM was going to make a big offer for the film rights to my novel. If that deal had not fallen through, we would have been able to bet on Truman. But if I had received a contract from MGM, we might have gone to Hollywood and I wouldn't have become involved in the Truman campaign." Have you thought about how you're going to feel if Truman actually makes it?" Barbara said. "Feel? I'll feel great—and we'll celebrate!"

We had been invited to an election party sponsored by the Democratic National Committee at a hotel in Washington, but we had decided that we would stay at our apartment in New York because we had to make final arrangements for our transfer to Boston.

"I guess I let the pollsters and Jonathan Daniels persuade me that I shouldn't even consider the idea that Truman could pull through," I said. "Daniels told me that if I identified with Truman I'd be torn apart when he lost. He didn't advise me on what to do if all the experts were wrong."

"He told you to keep cool," Barbara said. "That's all you have to do. Keep calm and realize that wonderful things are ahead for us." "I have you and Terry," I said. "That's all I need." "You do have us and we have you," she said. "But you have more than that. You have friends in Boston and New York and Washington who know how many abilities you have. You have a book that's going to get good reviews in many places. You have nothing to worry about." "I have to take care of my family," I said. "You love us and we love you," Barbara answered. "Terry and I are ready to go wherever you go."

We went to bed joyfully that night. I thought we were prepared for any surprises we might encounter in the years to come.

CHAPTER SEVEN

THE PRESIDENT STUNS THE EXPERTS—AND I PREPARE FOR A NEW LIFE

AS THE VOTES WERE BEING COUNTED across the country on the night of November 2, Barbara and I were doing final packing for our journey to New England. We had placed many of our small possessions in a trunk and had dispatched it to Boston. We didn't own many things at that stage of our lives. We could easily cram clothing and paperback books into three suitcases.

We turned on our radio at 9 o'clock to hear the early returns. I braced myself for an announcement of a Dewey sweep, but the announcer said: "President Truman is doing better than any of the polls predicted. Not many ballots have been tabulated yet, but he is showing more strength than any one expected...."

I looked at Barbara. "Maybe we should have gone to Washington, to be with our friends," I said. "Maybe there will be something to celebrate." "You didn't want to be at a gloomy party, surrounded by sad people," she reminded me. "You thought it would be too painful."

The complexities of a national election baffled me. I knew that Truman was gaining ground, but reports from many places indicated that millions of voters were undecided, confused, reluctant to make a choice. How could any ordinary citizen know which man in the race would be the wisest person to have in the White House in a time of rapid changes? Many citizens had never had any personal contacts with Truman or Dewey or Henry Wallace or Strom Thurmond. Their judgments had to be made on their responses to campaign speeches, newsreels, articles in newspapers, or radio programs.

The voices on our radio in New York began to get louder. The announcers lost their cool tones. They didn't seem able to understand or interpret the results pouring in.I heard one man proclaim, "Truman is leading Governor Dewey by more than one million votes, but Dewey's campaign manager still expects Dewey to overtake Truman as more returns are counted...." A broadcaster named H. V. Kaltenborn, with a heavy Germanic accent, asserted that Truman would be badly beaten. Another announcer declared that Henry Wallace was getting hundreds of thousands of votes on the American Labor Party ticket in New York— votes that might have gone to Truman if Wallace had not been in the race.

We had one bottle of wine left in our apartment. We opened it, filled our glasses, and drank a toast to Harry Truman. I said, "Even if he goes down, he is making a damned good showing. I'm glad you urged me to work for him." Barbara sipped her wine. Her eyes were twinkling with delight. "I hope Shelby put some money on the President."

Suddenly we heard a man screeching on the radio: "I don't know how it's going to go, folks, but it looks now as though only Truman can win!" I jumped up. "It sounds as though that guy is losing his mind." Barbara began to dance around the room. "Maybe he is, darling. Maybe a lot of people will lose their minds tonight."

"My God, it's happening," I said, sinking down on the couch in our living room. "I'm as dumb as those correspondents in Boston. I heard the roar of that crowd and I knew that people were swinging to Truman and then I thought of what Jonathan Daniels told me. He reminded me that I'd never been in a campaign before. He didn't want me to be carried away."

Barbara pulled me to my feet. "Let's dance! Let us be happy this night. This is a great night. It's a great night for Harry and everybody who worked for him. You did your part. We'll have our own celebration." I wasn't able to dance. We sat down again and had a little more wine.

"Here we are, getting ready to go to Boston," I groaned. "And the action is down in Washington. I shouldn't have listened to Daniels or the other wise guys who told me Truman couldn't make it." I had believed in my heart that Truman was a champion. But I had been crippled by fear—the fear of taking a long chance, the fear of falling on my face, the fear of leading my friends down the wrong road.

Barbara held me tight. "When you took the Boston University job, you made the best decision you could," she said. "You wanted to take care of me and take care of Terry. The Truman people thought you weren't interested in staying in politics. They regarded you as a writer and a teacher." "After that Winchell item I knew I couldn't hope to get an appointment from Truman," I said. "I closed the door on that idea."

The shouting on the radio was getting louder. Voices from New York and Chicago and Los Angeles—from all around the nation—expressed amazement at the growing size of Truman's margin: "The biggest upset in American political history.... The experts missed the groundswell for Truman.... The Democrats are regaining control of the House and the Senate.... How did Truman do it?...." An announcer said: "The President is not available for comment. He is not in his home in Independence, and reporters can't find him...."

"Maybe he wasn't sure that he could pull it off, after all," I speculated. "Why didn't he spend this night with Bess and Margaret and some of his friends? He must have gone somewhere with a few Secret Service men."

"I believe he went to a private place where he could think quietly about his responsibilities," Barbara said. "He didn't want to be hounded by the newspaper men. You don't blame him, do you?" "No, I don't," I said. "He doesn't owe them anything." Then I realized I should have considered what the victory meant to Truman, the nation, and the world. I had been focusing on myself and my part in it.

The liberal promises Truman had made in his speeches might be embodied in proposals for the next Congress—a Democratic Congress, with new leaders. Truman was no longer the man who had stepped into Roosevelt's shoes. He was the President elected by the people of the United States. He could go far beyond Roosevelt.

I rose to my feet again. "Here's a toast to Harry, wherever he is," I said, clinking my wine glass against hers. "Here's hoping that he will be the greatest president we've ever had." I wished then I hadn't been so anxious about our expenses. I should have scraped together enough money to take Barbara and Terry to Washington, especially for the final month. The Batts and the Birkheads asked me often about her and Terry. We could have had some joyful evenings together. I had deprived her of the opportunity to be there—to share what the rest of us were going through.

Yet she had persuaded me to make the leap into Truman's struggle. Her steady faith and love had sustained me during those exhausting months. She had never wavered in her belief that the whole effort was worthwhile. "You were very lucky," she said, "and you are still luckier than you realize. We may not be in the celebration in Washington, but we are going to have a great time in Boston. Your students will love you and your book is going to get wonderful reviews."

Then she paused, as though she wondered whether she should tell me what had come into her mind, and she spoke in a quick burst, "And you may be asked to go back to Washington, too. I have a feeling you will have many more things to do there." "I'm not expecting that," I said. "But whatever happens we were in a campaign nobody will forget. Nobody can take that away from us."

On the morning of November 3, 1948, we walked around our little apartment, remembering the years we had lived together there. We had been married on December 5, 1941—just two days before the Japanese attack on Pearl Harbor—and we had spent our honeymoon in that place. We had kept our lease on it for seven years, subletting it to friends during the war and returning to it after my service in the army. We had decided to keep it as our New York residence as long as we could.

Terry looked up into our faces as we went around the small rooms. He was not certain of what was going to happen to us when we left there. We lifted him for reassuring hugs. We told him that we had rented a house near Boston and that we would have neighbors who had children—so he would have playmates. "There'll be lots of snow," I said. "We'll make snow men in our back yard. You'll have a sled and I'll take you for a ride on the snow."

We carried our suitcases from Patchin Place over to Sixth Avenue and a cruising taxi stopped for us. We rode through the morning traffic to Grand Central Station. A black porter took our bags and put them on a luggage cart.

As we walked along with the porter I said to him: "Well, Truman did it, he surprised everybody, didn't he?" The porter gave me an appraising glance. "I don't know how you feel about it," he said. "But it's a big day for people like me. Truman was for civil rights, man. Everybody I know voted for him." "So did we," I said, when he had loaded our suitcases on board the train. He accepted the money I gave him and flashed a smile. "Then it's a good day for you, too," he said.

Then I was glad Hubert Humphrey had fought for a strong civil rights plank in the Democratic platform and I was glad that Truman had referred often to that plank in his speeches. Truman had lost a few Southern states, but he had gained the votes of 90 per cent of the black citizens in the major cities in the states he had needed for his victory.

The train went smoothly and swiftly toward Boston. Barbara and I talked about how Truman had pulled together a coalition of people from many backgrounds. "I'd like to look at the tabulations," I said. "But I think it was mainly the blacks, the labor union members, and the veterans who decided to support Harry."

"And women," Barbara added. "Mary Abbott and I weren't alone. He's obviously a good man, a brave man, true to what he believes, true to his wife. He is a kind and compassionate man."

"But he was pretty rough on his opponents," I said. "He accused them of helping the rich and sticking knives into the backs of the poor. He declared that the Republicans in Congress had passed an anti-Semitic, anti-Catholic law, dealing with displaced persons. He said they were bad and cynical. He wasn't very kind to the Republicans." Barbara nodded. "Yes, he was rough on them. Maybe a little too rough. I don't know whether they were as bad as he said they were. But I think he believed they were pretty bad—and he wanted the people to know about them."

I can't remember all the things Barbara and I talked about while the train went through the New England towns. I don't recall that we felt sorry for Tom Dewey or Henry Wallace or Strom Thurmond, the losers. I'm sure we didn't anticipate the troubles Truman would have to face from the Republicans who had retained their seats in Congress. We didn't realize that the bitterness of the campaign would endure for decades.

On the journey to Boston on that bright November day, Barbara and I hoped that Truman's triumph would bring many benefits to the people of our country and the world. We hoped that partisanship would be put aside—and that the members of the newly elected Congress would work constructively with the President to maintain peace and to solve the problems which demanded well-planned solutions.

The Berlin blockade was still in effect. The Soviets were still trying to drive the United States, Britain, and France out of West Germany. The United Nations was endangered by that conflict. The possibility of war threatened our lives and the lives of people everywhere. Millions of refugees were living on the edge of starvation. Millions of veterans were trying to find homes for their newly-formed families.

Our two-year-old son gazed eagerly through the wide windows of the railroad car in which he rode. But he couldn't stay in the seat with us for very long. He was an explorer, running up and down the aisle. After two or three hours he became tired. He climbed into Barbara's lap and went to sleep.

"I'm looking forward to being in a house again," Barbara said. "Patchin Place was fine for the two of us, but Terry needs to be in a house and have a yard to play in." I had spent my early years in a house, and so had Barbara. We wanted to give our son the home which would be best for him.

At the suggestion of a Boston University faculty member, we had rented a small house in Stoughton, a town about thirty miles from Boston. It was one of a row of new houses, not far from a railroad station. It had a modern kitchen and radiant heating in the floor. The back yard was fairly large. It would certainly be better for a child than our New York apartment had been.

"It will be cold in Boston this winter," I said. "But it can't be as icy as the one we went through when we were there in the war." Barbara shivered. We remembered the savage winter of 1942-43, when I had been a Nieman Fellow. Blizzards battered New England with howling fury. Nazi submarines sank tankers off the Atlantic coast, and there wasn't enough fuel oil to keep buildings warm. We had an apartment on Chauncy Street, a few blocks from the Harvard Yard, but we were chilled there even though we wore long underwear and heavy coats.

"There'll be plenty of snow," Barbara said. "We can count on that." "At least this time we won't freeze," I said. "We'll step out of bed every morning on a toasted floor." "If that radiant heating is as good as they say it is," Barbara murmured. Then her eyes sparkled. "And we won't be there very long. You'll get an offer you can't refuse. You'll accept it because you like to keep moving, and you know Terry and I are ready to go anywhere with you."

I had gone from job to job and we had moved from city to city. But I was positive that I would have to stay in Boston for a while, because I had made commitments to the university and to the editors of the Atlantic Monthly Press.

"I'll have to stay at the university for a couple of years," I said. "The dean and the faculty gave me a special appointment. I can't let them down, and I've promised to start another novel soon." "You can do that easily," Barbara said. "Write one about Truman. The man who was declared to be politically dead—and came to life again."

"It's too early for that," I answered. "I don't understand what happened. People will be trying to figure it out as long as we live—and after we've gone. Maybe Terry will understand it when he grows up."

"You don't have to understand it," Barbara said. "Concentrate on the man who changed your life and the lives of all of us. This man went out and faced a whole nation. He went throughout the country, calling to the people, asking them to act for their own best interests. He told them he was a servant, a hired hand, and he promised them he would do what needed to be done."

"I'll think about it," I said, looking through the window as the train rushed toward Boston. "I want to forget about Washington for a long while. I'm going to be a professor. I'll buy a tweed jacket with patched elbows. I'll learn to smoke a pipe. I'll stroll around the campus, looking at all the beautiful students."

"You mean all the beautiful girls," Barbara said, frowning. "I hope you won't have any in your classes." "You don't have anything to worry about," I said, pulling her close. "You are more beautiful than any girl I might ever see in any class." Sitting beside her in the speeding train, gazing at my sleeping son, I felt a surge of gratitude for all that Barbara had brought into my life. I had never expected to be married to such a gifted person. She had accepted me as a moody writer, as a journalist, as a politician, and finally as a teacher. Now she was willing to have me play the role of a professor.

The train arrived in Boston. Terry awakened with a startled cry. We hugged him and hugged one another. Whatever happened, we would be together.

I thought I was beginning a new life—a life of scholarship and leisure, a life with plenty of hours in which to write, a life in which I would lead my students joyfully through the fields of learning. I wouldn't be a ghost any more, hidden in a dusty office, writing speeches for another man to deliver. I would have my own identity.

CHAPTER EIGHT

IN THE TIDE OF TRUMAN'S TRIUMPH, I AM PULLED BACK TO WASHINGTON

THREE DAYS AFTER WE ARRIVED IN BOSTON, I realized I was involved in the consequences of the political earthquake Truman had brought about. I was asked to explain his victory at a public meeting of students and faculty members at Boston University.

Striding into my office, the dean of the School of Communications said, "Elmo Roper had accepted our invitation to comment on the election and tell us what we could expect from President Dewey. He sent us a telegram, saying that he couldn't be here. Now everybody wants to hear about how Truman won—and what he is likely to do next. Since you worked on his campaign, we're sure that you can illuminate the situation. People are eager to hear what you have to say." "I'm not eager to speak," I answered. "What kinds of questions will I be asked?"

"Will Truman really fight for the programs he advocated in his speeches? Will he push for a national health plan? How much federal money will he pour into education?" The dean paused, and then added, "Will he battle for civil rights? More opportunities for women? More housing for veterans? Those are questions that concern all of us here."

"And you expect me to answer those questions right off the bat?" I said. The dean looked at me. "You were with him all the way," the dean said. "His campaign oratory was evidently effective. You had a hand in it. Was much of it just the usual rhetoric? Or did he mean it? You can certainly talk about those things."

"I know about the priorities we had in the campaign," I said. "I can talk about that. I can tell the students and faculty that Truman will try to do exactly what he declared he would do. He's going beyond Roosevelt's New Deal. He'll face a lot of opposition in Congress."

A few days later I walked into an auditorium filled with students and teachers. It seemed to me there were thousands of them, stretching as far as I could see. I had never faced an audience of that size; I seized the lectern with trembling hands. I thought of all the crowds Truman had confronted, week after week, and I appreciated his bravery and endurance more than ever.

I spoke from notes, without using a prepared text. I didn't think I was qualified—or anyone was yet qualified—to describe the complexities and scope of the campaign. I described the meetings in the White House, the daily grind of members of the Research Division, the telephone calls we made to people in the towns along the routes traveled by the President's train, the way in which we inserted local references so that the people in each place would realize that Truman was aware of their problems, their accomplishments, and their view of the future. I mentioned I was often asked to do drafts of short speeches on housing, because I had been an information specialist for the National Housing Agency. I also contributed ideas and sentences for speeches on many other topics.

As an example of our operations, I quoted from a memorandum dated October 4, 1948, sent to five of us by Bill Batt. He informed us: "The President likes it best when we take a single theme for a single day and develop different phases of the theme throughout the day. If the area is agricultural, the short speeches should be written about the best issues in the agricultural field—rural housing, farm price supports, the Rural Electrification Agency, etc. If it is labor, each of the short speeches should be devoted to one of the good issues in that field—i.e., minimum wages, full employment, the Taft-Hartley law, attacks on the Labor Department, etc...." In the week between October 4 and October 11, each of us had to draft seven speeches. Our drafts were sent by plane to a city where the train stopped. The speeches were than given to George Elsey, who looked them over, added touches of his own, and gave them to the President for delivery from the back platform of the train.

"Truman assumed American voters had an insatiable appetite for facts," I said. "What were the facts about the situation in Europe? How did the conflicts between the United States and the Soviets arise? How could Americans attain the highest standard of living in the world—and help other people to rise from poverty? Why was it important for the federal government to provide aid to schools and colleges? How could be protect our environment and conserve our natural resources? We tried to answer all of those questions—and many more."

In my talk that day in Boston, I suppose I placed too much emphasis on the contributions that came from those of us in the Research Division. There were undoubtedly other factors which led to Truman's electoral victory. Dewey and Wallace and Thurmond—his principal opponents—could not match Truman's energy and determination. They did not have the resources of the White House at their disposal.

In a book entitled *Beyond the New Deal: Harry S. Truman and American Liberalism,* historian Alonzo Hamby declared: "The Research Division was actually an extension of the liberal caucus within the administration, serving essentially as its staff." I did not think of myself as a "liberal" or regard the Division as the staff of a "caucus"—an inner committee connected to Truman and his advisors. I thought of myself - and the other members of the Division—as citizens who had been asked to use their talents to serve a President who had to make a thorough and convincing case for his election.

I made it clear to the audience in Boston that I had become utterly convinced the 1948 battle was not simply a contest in which candidates tried to stack up the largest piles of votes. It was a fierce combat between fundamental forces in American society. I felt I had been fortunate to serve with Truman's crusade for justice—fair treatment for everyone in a vast nation.

When I ended my talk, students and faculty members stood and applauded. Many of them had evidently voted for Truman and were delighted by what had happened. Several students came up to me and asked whether I would be appointed to a position on the White House staff. I explained to them I had not plunged into the campaign with any expectation of an appointment from Truman. I said I expected to be teaching and writing in Boston for a long time. I told them about my forthcoming novel and expressed my hope they would want to get copies. They were keenly interested in the book.

Three days after I made that speech, I received a telephone call from Stephen Fitzgerald, a friend of mine who had formed a public relations agency in New York. He congratulated me on Truman's victory and then informed me he had a client in Boston who needed the services of a professional writer. He offered me a substantial fee to help his client and to become a consultant to his agency.

I discussed Fitzgerald's offer with the dean, who told me he did not think the university would have any objection to any outside work I did—so long as it did not raise ethical questions or interfere with my teaching. I needed the additional income, because my starting salary as an associate professor was only $4,800 a year—much less than the amount I had been paid as an Assistant Director of the Research Division in Washington. I called Fitzgerald and reached an agreement with him.

Before I had any other communications from Fitzgerald, another offer came to me—one that pleased me and tempted me. The dean's secretary told me, "A Senator with a funny name called you from Washington." She added, "I didn't write it down, because he said he would call again." "If he does call and I'm not around, please write it down," I said, "I'd like to know what he wants."

Two days later, she handed me a note. She had written: "Please call Senator Scott Lucas." There was a telephone number under his name. When I called that number, I remembered I had drafted a speech for Senator Lucas in the special session of Congress after Truman had summoned the legislators back to Washington in July. I remembered I had sat next to Al Vigderman, an assistant to Lucas, during the deliberations of the platform committee in Philadelphia.

The Senate telephone operator in Washington connected me with the office of Senator Lucas. When I gave my name, Vigderman came on the line, "Do you really want to stay up there and freeze this winter in Boston, Frank Kelly? We'd like to have you come back here and help us save the country."

"We've already saved the country," I answered. "I've just started as a professor, Al. I've promised my students I'll be with them for a while. They're helping me to learn how to be a teacher and I'm getting paid for it, too." "Listen to me, man," Vigderman said sharply. "You helped Harry Truman to get elected. You're obliged to help him get his program through Congress. You know that Alben Barkley becomes Vice President in January. When Barkley leaves the Senate, Scott Lucas becomes the Majority Leader. He needs an assistant with some brains and an ability to write. He's dreaming of becoming President some day, too."

"He has plenty of good assistants," I said. "He has you and Margaret McMahon and other bright people on his staff." "We have to help him be an effective Senator as well as a Majority Leader," Vigderman said. "You know how big Illinois is. There are millions of people who count on him."

I knew there were tremendous demands on a Senator from a large and heavily populated state. Lucas was a senior member of several of the important committees. He had to attend many hearings. As Majority Leader and chairman of the Majority Policy Committee, he would have a dominant role in forming the agenda of the Senate.

"He'll have a separate office in the Capitol when he takes over Barkley's leadership position," Vigderman said. "He needs a special assistant there. Being a Majority Leader is a tough job." "I know it is," I said. "It's important and I'd like to work with him, but I've made a commitment to the university here."

"Truman can't get anything through the Senate without the Majority Leader's advice and consent," Vigderman went on. "You and I can guide Scott Lucas. He's going to be in a crossfire between the Southerners and the Northern liberals led by Hubert Humphrey. He'll need all the help we can give him."

"There must be people who would jump at the chance to be a special assistant to the Senate's leader," I said. "It must be a very interesting spot. But I can't just jump away from my place here. What do I tell the dean—or Dr. Marsh, the president of the university?" "Tell them Truman needs you more than they do," Vigderman said. "Get a leave of absence. You can always go back to teaching."

I didn't think Dr. Marsh would be likely to give me a leave on such short notice. And I didn't know whether Truman needed me or not. After his victory, thinking of all the people who had worked for him, I felt my part was very small. "I can't tell the dean or Dr. Marsh that Truman is demanding my return to Washington," I said, laughing. The truth was that Al Vigderman and I had worked together well in Philadelphia. I was sure he was largely responsible for any interest Senator Lucas might have in me.

"Al, you're a very persuasive man," I said. "But I can't let you talk me into quitting my job here and rushing back to Washington. I'm sure that you and the Senator can find another man for that position." "Let me put the Senator on the phone," Vigderman answered. "You'll hit it off with him." Senator Lucas had a warm, pleasant voice. He asked me to come to Washington as soon as possible for a talk with him. "We've just moved to Boston," I said. "The strain of moving is hard on my wife."

"Al told me she encouraged you to write speeches for Truman," Senator Lucas said. "His election won't mean much if we can't get his proposals through the Senate and the House. We're in for a hard fight, Professor Kelly. I've talked to Charlie Murphy and Clark Clifford on the White House staff. They think you could help us."

I was stirred by that. I hadn't heard from anybody in the White House since the election. I thought I was a forgotten man. "Even if my wife accepts the idea, it will be difficult for me to ask Dr. Marsh to let me leave his faculty so quickly," I muttered. "If we come to an agreement, I'll call Dr. Marsh and ask him to release you for service here," Senator Lucas said. "When can you get down here?" I told him that I would call him again after a consultation with my wife.

I suppose I felt flattered by the statements Vigderman and Lucas made. When I reported those conversations to Barbara her eyes widened with astonishment. "I knew you'd get an offer, but I don't think you should accept this one," she said. "I don't want to have us move again, but that's a small point. Can you turn your back on the people at Boston University? The Atlantic Monthly Press editors are expecting you to start another book. Will you have time to write novels in Washington? If Senator Lucas decides to run for president, will we be involved in another campaign? Are you going to be a professional politician?"

"First of all, let me remind you that you persuaded me to work for Truman," I answered. "Do we have any obligation to help him get his program passed by Congress? Don't you think that's important?"

"It's important if you think it is absolutely essential for you to be in the fight," she said. "You're a writer. You have many things to say—the possibility of many books. Isn't that important, too? And what about your promise to the president of the university? You told some students that you planned to teach here for years to come."

I realized then I wanted to do many things at once. I wanted to be on Capitol Hill, at the right hand of the Majority Leader of the Senate. I wanted to be writing books. I also wanted to be teaching students—and learning from them.

"I guess I'm an activist," I said. "I guess I've convinced myself that Truman and Lucas really need my help. I didn't have any ambition to be in politics. You know that. But I worked on so many speeches about the problems of the country and the world. I feel that I have to do what I can. It's important for all of us to keep the Republicans from wrecking everything." She circled me with her arms. "If you feel that way, I can see that we'll be going back to Washington. Terry and I know you care about us."

I went over to the offices of the Atlantic Monthly Press and told Charlie Morton that I felt an obligation to return to Washington if I reached an agreement with Senator Lucas. He rose to his feet in anger, and said, "The Boston University people will think you're crazy! You can't abandon your place on the faculty. You should stay here and get started on another book. You should write three more books as fast as you can. It takes three or four novels for a writer to get recognized. You'll lose your momentum if you get into the political quagmire. It could ruin you."

"I've got to help Truman if I can," I said. "He's facing some tough fights." "You've already helped him," Morton answered. "You're not obliged to do anything more."

"I want to help Truman carry out his campaign promises," I said. "I put some of those promises into speeches for him. Roosevelt and Truman opened up a lot of avenues for me. I want to do more than I've done."

Morton paced across his office. "You don't care about your students? You don't care about being a professor at a good university? You don't care about being a novelist whose books may have more effects on people than any political actions?"

Those questions rattled me. After a minute of thinking, I responded, "I do care. I know the university is a great place. I wish I could stay here to write and teach—and go to Washington, too. But I think I can write there. The experience will be valuable to me as a writer."

Morton shook his head. "You already have enough experience to do as many books as you can produce in one lifetime, Kelly. How much experience do you need? You're going to change the direction of your life if you go down there." "I didn't seek any Washington job," I said. "I planned to stay here."

Morton had taken the initiative to get me appointed to the university faculty. I had not sought that appointment. I didn't remind him of the small size of my salary or tell him I had never expected to be a college professor. In fact, he had arranged the appointment with an expectation that my primary work would be the production of books for the Atlantic Monthly Press. "Maybe the Washington experience will be useful if I return to teaching some day," I said.

Morton's face flushed. "You'll never be able to get on a college faculty again if you make this jump. You can make a living as a journalist or as a novelist. But I don't believe you could think about teaching again." "I'm sorry, Charlie," I said. I'm grateful to you and I guess I've let you down. Your friends at the university will think I'm a jackass."

Morton sat down at his desk and stared at a stack of manuscripts. "I thought you had the perfect set-up here in Boston—with the prestige of a professor and plenty of time to write stories and books. You'd have every summer free, to write or to travel."

I wondered then whether he had always had a hankering to be a professor and to live a leisurely academic life. He spoke of it with such appreciation. Yet he had to confront the reality of what he had done— pushed me into a situation he regarded as ideal. But he hadn't counted on the possibility of a call from Washington.

"Don't worry about the people at the university," he said slowly. "They know I'm responsible for bringing you here. I'll take the heat for your departure." Then he smiled, and said, "We didn't think little Harry Truman could possibly win. He fooled us." After a pause he added sharply, "I still think he isn't up to the job. But none of the other candidates were worth a vote either. I thought the election should have been a scoreless tie."

"If you spent an hour with Truman, you'd feel differently," I said. "He's an honest man and a good man. He'll have a high place in our history." Morton shrugged. "At least he picked you and some other bright guys to write a lot of his speeches. I'll give him credit for that."

"He went out and faced millions of people," I said. "He convinced them he was the best man available for the White House job. It wasn't simply the power of words that brought him the victory. It was his own character that spoke for him." "And he was lucky enough to run against Dewey and Wallace and Thurmond," Morton muttered. "Who could vote for one of those guys?"

After a moment, Morton came over and put a hand on my right shoulder. He gazed intensely at me. "You want to make history," he said. "I might want to do it at your age. I suppose you'll be working for an honest Senator. But watch out for some of them. They'll try to corrupt you."

Then he glanced at me critically. "You've got to dress better if you're going to be the assistant to the Senate Majority Leader," Morton admonished me. "You'll need a tailor-made suit. I'll take you over to J. Press in Cambridge and get you fitted for one. If you're going to hang around with Senators, you can't look like a sloppy newspaperman or an absent-minded professor."

The idea seemed absurd to me. I had never had any interest in expensive clothes or making an impression by my appearance. But Morton insisted on taking me to the J. Press Tailors in Cambridge. He picked out a closely woven dark fabric with a gold pinstripe in it. With that material, the price of the suit came to $150—several times more than I had ever paid for a suit before. I had less than $400 in the bank and it struck me as extravagant to buy such a suit. Barbara, who had been trying to get me to wear better clothes, thought it was a good investment.

Wearing my costly garment, I traveled to Washington for a series of talks with Lucas, Vigderman and Margaret McMahon, the senator's administrative assistant. I noticed Lucas and Vigderman were wearing fashionable suits, and I realized they appreciated my splendid apparel. Later, Vigderman told me the Senator had commented favorably on my tailoring. Lucas indicated I looked more like a banker than a professor, but he was sure we would get along well together.

Lucas informed me he intended to be a very active Majority Leader. He hoped I would be willing to work with him six or seven days a week. He planned to make many statements in the Senate and in press conferences. I sensed he had an inner ambition to be a candidate for President when Truman retired. At the conclusion of our conversations, he asked me to come to Washington early in January. He announced he would call Dr. Marsh and ask for my release from Boston University's faculty.

"I think Dr. Marsh will be aware of the fact I am offering you a very important job," Lucas said. "You will be serving your country. He should be happy to have one of his faculty members in such a position." "I don't know whether he regards any other job as more important than being on his faculty," I said. "In any case, I'll be with you in January."

When I returned to Boston, I went to see Dr. Marsh. It was immediately clear he did not share the Senator's feeling that serving the Senate had a higher value than teaching at the university. He looked at me with sorrow and dismay. He reminded me I had been appointed an associate professor, with the likelihood of promotion to full professor and permanent tenure. He could not understand why I was willing to toss away all those advantages.

"Life in politics is often subject to painful changes," Dr. Marsh said, with the air of a man explaining obvious things to me. "I was told by Charles Morton that you did not want to be a professional politician.

Why do you want to plunge into that morass? Do you really believe you will find deep satisfaction in an atmosphere of deals and compromises?"

"Truman has offered proposals that will be good for education, good for the country, good for the world," I said. "What happens in Washington affects the future of all of us. The Senate will be a battleground. I can't stay out of the battle." Dr. Marsh examined me with a piercing glance. "You are chasing a will-o'-the-wisp," he said, after a moment. "You won't be happy in politics. You got into the presidential campaign as a writer. You may be disgusted when you find out what goes on in the Senate. It won't be a lofty struggle."

"I may be making a mistake," I said. "I may be disappointed. I'm sorry I can't stay here. I've enjoyed my time with the students. It's a fine university. I may never get a chance to return to teaching. But I have to do what I think is right." Dr. Marsh nodded. "Yes, I certainly agree with that. I wish you well and I hope that you will accomplish what you are determined to do. I am glad that you realize that you are burning your bridges here. I had my doubts about appointing you—and I wish I had paid heed to my doubts." "I understand how you feel," I said.

I realized I had been too hasty in accepting a place on his faculty. Because I had not received any other offers while I was working for Truman, I had doubted my ability to find a good position. I had not fully considered the consequences of my decision to follow the course Charlie Morton had recommended to me.

I had always been willing to jump from one field to another, to gather experience in many ways, to examine new options, to risk new ventures. I loved being a journalist, but I wanted to do more than chronicle the events of my time. I found it stimulating to be a teacher, to shape young minds, to engage in the never-ending process of learning with my students, but I did not want to spend my remaining years in a classroom. I wanted to change the world. In Washington, I might be a mover and a shaker.

Barbara had frequently urged me to make plans, to outline my life in a series of steps, to think of where I might be in three years or five years or ten. But I couldn't do that. I liked to go with the flow. Although

I had become a husband and a father, I wasn't ready to settle down. I wanted to swim in the fast-moving stream of life.

I was exhilarated by the power of words—the power Truman had used to keep his place at the head of the government. When I heard Truman speaking words I had written for him, I was stirred by the thought of the impact such words might have. In Washington, words were instruments to create changes—not simply employed for communication. I knew I could handle words, and that ability would give me power.

I remembered a brief encounter I had with President Roosevelt in the Oval Office in April of 1938. At the invitation of a Washington correspondent I had attended one of his press conferences. He radiated the confidence of a man who had altered the fundamental conditions of life for millions of people. The reporters hung on his words.

After the conference I was introduced to him as a young man who had just entered journalism. Roosevelt gave me a warm handshake, his eyes twinkling. He said, "I thought of being a reporter when I was young, Mr. Kelly. Perhaps I missed my calling." I had the nerve to tell him, "You're doing pretty well in your present job, Mr. President." He laughed and responded, "I'm glad you think so."

It was evident to me then that Franklin Roosevelt had made the right choice when he passed over journalism to go into politics. He might have been a great reporter, but he couldn't have accomplished all the things he was able to do as a public leader. He was a masterful communicator as well as a politician. So I was sure he didn't actually feel he might have missed his "calling."

I had never felt particularly called to be a journalist or a professor. I had a continuing urge to delve into every area of life, to uncover the deepest meanings of existence, to see everything and know everything. I believe I wanted to be God—to be in command of this universe and any other realms that might be beyond the farthest galaxies. My life had been altered by the hidden powers that moved the stars and the planets and all the creatures shaped by that divinity. I thought I had made my own decisions, but in retrospect I wondered whether I had been as free as I considered myself to be.

If I had stayed in Boston, I might have become an established member of the academic world. I might also have produced a string of novels. I might have become a respected writer as well as a noted professor, and I might have been happier in a hundred ways. But that kind of life had not been designed for me.

So I went back to Washington—to do what I thought I had been called to do. I soon ran into the hard complexities of a government dominated by suspicious men. I encountered the walls that separated Senators from one another, the walls that separated the Congress from the White House and the Supreme Court, the walls that separated the federal institutions from the people. I discovered it was very difficult to get anything accomplished while many people worked day and night for conflicting purposes.

I learned that the enormously complicated structures created by the Founding Fathers of the United States prevented swift action—and often blocked any action at all. I saw a President cheerfully shouldering responsibilities that were actually too much for any man to bear. He never accepted any defeat as final—and I tried to follow his example.

CHAPTER NINE

INAUGURATED WITH IMPERIAL SPLENDOR, TRUMAN SPEAKS TO THE WORLD AS A HUMBLE MAN

WHEN HARRY TRUMAN had taken his first oath of office as President in April of 1945, he had been pale and shaken. It had been a time of sorrow, with the nation focused upon the sudden death of his predecessor. But in January 1949, when he was inaugurated for a full term in his own right, he was bronzed and healthy, a vibrant man at the center of the most magnificent celebration Washington had ever seen.

A million people had poured into the city to watch his inaugural parade, but television cameras carried views of it to an estimated 10 million persons. Radio networks were prepared to transmit his words to more than 100 million listeners in the United States and other countries. More people would hear Truman's twangy voice than had heard the voices of all the preceding Presidents. The United States was the most powerful country on earth and people everywhere wanted to hear what the man from Missouri had to say.

It was a glorious day for Captain Harry and for all of us who had helped him to achieve his electoral victory. I was one of the invited guests who sat in the Capitol Plaza, facing the stand where he took the oath from Chief Justice Fred Vinson of Kentucky, a former Congressman who had been appointed by Truman to preside over the Supreme Court. I sat next to a jubilant black man, Walter White, a leader of the National Association for the Advancement of Colored People, who insisted that black voters in the nation's big cities deserved much of the credit for Truman's triumph. Thousands of African Americans had come to Washington for the celebration. Many of them had been able to stay at previously segregated hotels, because Truman had ordered his inaugural committee to secure equal treatment for all citizens in the capital.

Truman's first words after the taking of his oath to uphold the Constitution were consistent with statements he had made to many audiences in his campaign—that he regarded himself as "a hired hand," a public servant in the White House. In the midst of the huge throng that day, he showed no signs of arrogance: "I accept with humility the honor which the American people have conferred on me," Truman said. "I accept it with a resolve to do all I can for the welfare of this nation and for the peace of the world...."

As I listened to him, I remembered what he had told a group of people in the Mayflower Hotel, "I was not in any way elated over the election... I felt only the responsibility, and that is what we are faced with now." He was always on guard against the temptation of being carried away by flattery or too much emphasis on a President's exalted status.

Although his awareness of the tremendous problems he faced certainly was evident on that bright blue day, Truman spoke vigorously and confidently about the future. He declared that democracy was the "vitalizing force" that would transform all nations. He cited four points as the major elements in the policies he would pursue: (1) strong support for the United Nations; (2) placing "full weight' behind the Marshall Plan to restore the economic strength of Western Europe; (3) forming a new "defense arrangement" among the North Atlantic countries; and (4) creating a "bold new program" for making the products of American science and industrial progress available to the "underdeveloped countries" where so many people suffered in poverty.

Truman made it clear that he did not advocate a return to imperialism—the exploitation of poor countries for profits. He reminded the attentive audience that half the people in the world were living in conditions that caused misery. He was sure that the United States could do much to change those conditions, without expending enormous sums of money. "The material resources which we can afford to use for assistance of other peoples are limited," Truman said. "But our imponderable resources in technical knowledge are constantly growing and are inexhaustible...."

As I heard Truman speak so eloquently about helping people all over the earth, I remembered how his opponents had dubbed him "the little guy" or "the hick from the cow country" or "the tool of Tom Pendergast" or "the bankrupt haberdasher." They had brushed aside his knowledge of the histories of many nations and his efforts to end poverty in the United States and the world.

After the President finished his speech, there was a display of national power which dazzled the people who stood in the streets of Washington. Hundreds of planes thundered across the sky, including five huge B-36 bombers. As the roar of the planes died away, Truman and the new Vice President, Alben Barkley, got into a limousine and went slowly down Pennsylvania Avenue, acknowledging the cheers of the watchers.

Veterans from Captain Harry's artillery battery in World War I— elderly men from Battery D, who had been in combat under Truman's command—walked beside the limousine, waving their canes and trying to keep in step with one another. Two of them became exhausted and had to drop out along the way, but the others marched briskly along to the gates of the White House.

My wife and I had seats in the President's Reviewing Stand that morning. With Truman and his aides, we were shielded by glass walls from the icy January wind. Truman had an electric heater near his feet, and he shifted nimbly from it when a short-circuit caused a brief fire which was quickly extinguished.

The parade extended for seven miles and took several hours to pass the White House. It was reported to be the longest inaugural procession in American history at that time. More than 15,000 men, women, and children took part in it, wearing all sorts of costumes. There were dozens of bands with blaring trumpets, beauty queens, trick riders, Marines, West Point cadets, midshipmen from the Naval Academy at Annapolis, companies of WACS (Women's Army Corps) and WAVES (women in naval service), four mules from Missouri, and a circus calliope playing the theme song of the inauguration: "I'm Just Wild About Harry."

Harry Truman may not have felt elated on the day of his election, but he certainly responded to the exuberant atmosphere of his inauguration. He laughed, shouted, beat time to the band music, smiled, clapped, and made crisp comments to Vice President Barkley and others who sat close to him. All of us who shared those flashing hours with him never forgot the exultance, the confidence, the beaming beneficence he radiated toward the paraders, the crowds in the streets, and the people around him.

In the surging excitement of that sunlit day, no one seemed to give much thought to the shadow of annihilation which had come upon the earth when Truman had authorized the use of atomic bombs on two Japanese cities, Hiroshima and Nagasaki. Truman had admitted that those weapons could bring unparalleled destruction upon humanity, but he believed that they could be brought under international control. He trusted the God of the Bible, and he was sure that his God had provided the means for his country to lead the people of the earth into a new era of lasting peace and prosperity.

In his address at the Capitol, he had asked for "the help and the prayers" of the thousands of citizens there. He acknowledged that he needed encouragement and support. He declared, "The tasks we face are difficult, and we can accomplish them only if we work together." He had been stingingly partisan in many of the speeches he delivered in his strenuous campaign, but on that day in January he did not strike a partisan note.

"It may be our lot to experience, and in a large measure to bring about, a major turning point in the long history of the human race," Truman said. "The first half of this century has been marked by unprecedented and brutal attacks on the rights of man, and by the two most frightful wars in history. The supreme need of our time is for men to learn to live together in peace and harmony."

In presenting his proposal to aid the "free peoples of the world," Truman emphasized the fact that he invited other countries "to pool their technological resources in this undertaking." He promised that the United States would do as much as it could, but insisted it would be vitally important for other nations to take part.

"This should be a cooperative enterprise in which all nations work together through the United Nations and its specialized agencies wherever practicable," Truman said. "It must be a world-wide effort for the achievement of peace, plenty, and freedom... Only by helping the least fortunate of its members to help themselves can the human family achieve the decent satisfying life that is the right of all people."

Although he denounced "the false philosophy that is communism"—and asserted that the United States would oppose it everywhere—Truman astonished many of his listeners by predicting that the people in the communist countries would eventually "abandon their delusions and join with the free nations of the world in a just settlement of internal differences."

In later years, Truman was accused of being one of the instigators of the "cold war" between Western nations and the Soviet-bloc countries. But it was evident in his inaugural address that he expected to see people bridging all the economic and ideological divisions. He concluded his address with an enormously optimistic statement, "With God's help the future of mankind will be assured in a world of justice, harmony and peace."

While I watched him in the reviewing stand that day—while the bands played and the happy marchers went swinging along Pennsylvania Avenue—I thought of the tremendous problems we faced. I was not sure the people of the United States—and the people of other countries—were prepared to act generously for the welfare of "the human family." Yet I admired Truman for speaking so boldly about the fundamental steps that had to be taken to create a global community. I saw a man with a growing mind and a developing soul, and I hoped that I could help him. Barbara and I went to the Inaugural Ball that night with David and Charlotte Lloyd, who had invited us to stay at their house for a few days. As one of Truman's administrative assistants, David had become an influential member of the White House staff. He had participated in the drafting of the inaugural speech, and he was deeply pleased by the strength of the President's delivery and responses of the crowd.

In a long conversation we had in his house that evening, David made it clear to us that it would be very hard to get many of Truman's proposals adopted. He spoke candidly and critically about Senator Lucas, the new Majority Leader. He made me wish I had given more thought to the problems I would have to face.

"Lucas is an easy-going, genial, middle-of-the-road Senator who wants to please everybody," David Lloyd said. "He doesn't stick his neck out very far. He is eager to get re-elected in 1950 and he'll trim his sails to appeal to every voter he can reach. He'll tell the President he'll fight for every bill we send to the Senate, but he won't fight long if the Southern Senators headed by Dick Russell are against him. I hope you can stiffen his backbone, Frank, but I doubt that anybody can do it."

Lloyd expressed some admiration for Richard Russell, the Senator from Georgia who was the chairman of the Armed Services Committee. He told me that Russell was well-balanced, highly intelligent, and friendly to Truman. He suspected that Russell wanted to be a presidential candidate in 1952—along with Lucas and a dozen other members of the Senate.

"Campaigns never end," Lloyd said. "Senators are always looking ahead a couple of years. Be aware of that. When you talk to a Senator, remember one thing: his main concern is to stay in the Senate. Every Senator believes his re-election is important for the whole country. He is reluctant to make any sacrifices, even to help a President of his own party."

"In his speech, Truman referred to the human family," I said. "Does he really feel related to everybody—or was that a line to catch every possible vote?" Lloyd laughed. "Didn't he make you feel related to him in the campaign, Frank? That's just the way he is. He has a genuine interest in everybody on this planet. When he decided to use atom bombs to end the war in 1945, he said he wanted to save Japanese lives as well as Americans. He meant it, too."

"Are there any Senators who think the way Truman does?" I said. "How are we going to get his program through the Senate?" Lloyd shrugged. "It's going to be tough—very tough. You didn't expect it to be easy, did you?"

When he saw that I was becoming depressed, Lloyd assured me he was glad I had accepted the appointment as the Majority Leader's assistant. He said that he was simply trying to prepare me for the situation in which I had to function. Barbara nodded several times while Lloyd talked about the selfishness of Senators. She felt that I had been too easily swayed by Al Vigderman and Scott Lucas. I had been in too much of a rush to get back to Washington.

"You shouldn't be downhearted, Frank," Lloyd said gently. "Truman knows what he is up against. He isn't daunted by it. We'll be knocked down in some of the fights ahead of us, but we'll get up again."

"If Congress balks, the President can always jump on a train and get voters to put the heat on their Senators and Representatives," I said. 'I suppose you plan to do that."

"He'll go to the country when he thinks it's necessary," Lloyd said. "But he will be trying to sell what he calls 'the fair deal'—and we don't know how many people will buy that if it gets stalled in the Congress." "They bought it in 1948," I said.

"They went for Harry Truman." Lloyd gave me a slow smile. "And we got the breaks, Frank. Dewey put on a miserable campaign. He separated himself from the Republican leaders in Congress and divided his own party. Strom Thurmond didn't have much appeal beyond the deep South. Henry Wallace stumbled around. People were finally convinced that Truman was a better man than his opponents, but that doesn't mean they accepted his program."

"People do know that Roosevelt's New Deal revived the country," I said. "Truman's program should appeal to everybody who supported Roosevelt."

"But Truman is calling for a national health insurance plan and a lot of doctors oppose that idea," Lloyd responded. "Truman is advocating civil rights laws that demand more than Roosevelt ever tried to get. He's asking for higher minimum wages, more unemployment compensation, higher benefits for veterans, more help for farmers, and long-range planning for public projects. The corporate lobbies are going to mobilize against us. Truman made enemies in the campaign and he'll make more, because he won't back down or give in to the lobbies."

I felt that the people would see the truth in what Truman had pointed out in his inaugural address: "All countries, including our own, will

113

greatly benefit from a constructive program for the better use of the world's human and natural resources." In that inspiring speech, Truman had declared that the rights of people in all countries had to be recognized in a fair system of economic and social cooperation. "If Truman gets people to understand what he's trying to do he'll have a big majority behind him," I said.

"I've been up against some of the lobbyists in this town and they're hard to beat," Lloyd said. "They have plenty of money. They can confuse and divide people. There are Senators and Representatives who rely on them and do what they want. And there are some Senators who are tigers; they'll spring on the President's back if they get a chance. They are dedicated to their own goals. They've seen Presidents come and go. They blocked Roosevelt many times. They can block Truman, too."

I knew David Lloyd had been the legislative director of the Americans for Democratic Action, an anti-Communist liberal organization founded in 1946 by men and women who had shaped Franklin Roosevelt's New Deal. The ADA had advocated extensions of Roosevelt's programs and had encountered strong opposition from the conservatives in the Congress. I understood how Lloyd felt about the reactionaries in the Senate.

"I came down here full of hope," I said. "I thought Truman had a lot of momentum." Lucas put one hand on my right shoulder. "You responded to a call," he said. "Charlie Murphy and Clark Clifford and I are going to keep in close touch with you. We encouraged Lucas to phone you. If you need help from the White House, call us. We'll certainly need your help when the Senate bogs down. But don't expect miracles. That's all I'm trying to tell you."

"It sounds as though we'll need a few miracles to get Truman's proposals enacted," I said. "We may get some," Lloyd answered quickly. "But don't count on them. Just remember that we'll be in one fight after another."

David Lloyd and his wife, Charlotte, were quietly religious people. They were both lawyers and both worked hard for the achievement of practical objectives. And they believed in the power of prayer. They had faith in God and in human beings. They had not succumbed to the cynicism which afflicted so many men and women in Washington.

In the subsequent years, from 1949 to 1952, as I became tormented and depressed by the savage infighting that went on in the Senate, Lloyd and I became close friends and allies in many struggles. I talked with him more often than with any other member of the White House staff. He was a gentle, courteous, responsive man who lived by a high code of ethics. The President and his associates had a deep respect for him.

I was thankful to Lloyd for his advice on many occasions. He helped me to understand the strange culture of the United States Senate—and to survive there for nearly four years. When his loyalty to his country was questioned by the demagogic Senator Joseph McCarthy, I obtained support for him from Hubert Humphrey and others who had the courage to expose the falsity of McCarthy's accusations. Truman staunchly defended Lloyd and others who were attacked by McCarthy.

In those years of anger and partisan strife, I was often sorry I had returned to Washington. I realized I was not suited to the bitter atmosphere of political life. In the Truman campaign I had been in the company of fine men who were as idealistic as I was. On Capitol Hill, such men existed but they were often defeated or personally damaged by the power-grabbers who prowled through the corridors of the Senate Office Buildings or behind the scenes in the Senate Chamber.

I had to take the consequences of decisions I had made. I felt that my life was going downhill, but I couldn't see any way to turn in a better direction. I became fully aware of what I should have known in 1948—that Truman's election had not opened the way for the great advances I had expected.

CHAPTER TEN

THE CRUSHING OF A DREAM—WHY THE TRUMAN PROGRAM WAS SMASHED IN THE CONGRESS

WHEN THE CHEERING for a victorious President came to a stop at the end of his inaugural party in 1949, the stalemate in American political life became evident again. The Senate and the House of Representatives were dominated by the conservative old men who had kept Franklin Roosevelt from extending the New Deal. Truman's proposals were knocked down, too. The battering was brutal in the Senate, which I found to be largely a racist, reactionary club.

In the years when I worked for the Majority Leader, struggling to get Truman's program enacted, the atmosphere was generally rancid. The committee chairmen were usually Southern Democrats, from states in which black voters and poor people seldom had access to the polling booths. There was no black man in the Senate. There was only one woman—Margaret Chase Smith of Maine, a thoughtful and intelligent Republican lady who was treated courteously but had no power.

Over and over again I had to face the reality of political conditions in America between 1949 and 1952. The election in 1948 of a majority of men who called themselves Democrats did not necessarily mean that the measures advocated by a liberal Democratic President would be enacted. The veteran Senators—who had been in office for dozens of years—guarded their privileges and prerogatives fiercely. The Majority leader had a limited influence upon them.

Truman was personally popular with most of them—and many Republicans as well, who respected his integrity—but he was seldom able to swing votes on domestic issues. His proposals were scrutinized in terms of how such legislation would affect the interests represented by the barons of the Senate. I wrote eloquent speeches for the Majority

116

Leader but I soon realized the tough old men who ran the Senate were not responsive to idealistic statements.

Staff members told me that many Senators—whether they were nominally Democrats or Republicans—were swayed by lobbyists or influential groups in their states. Many did not have time to study the issues on which they had to cast votes, so they relied on reports prepared for them by "specialists." Senators could rarely function as independent legislators, considering bills thoroughly and impartially. Some of them—perhaps fifteen or twenty, based on estimates given to me by journalists and fellow Senators—did have enough prestige and financial independence (as well as solid ethical principles) to vote in accordance with their consciences. The others shifted back and forth in the prevailing winds.

In the speeches we had drafted for Truman during his national campaign, we had given the highest priority to what seemed best for the country as a whole. But each member of the United States Senate served as a Senator from a particular state. In the debates in the cavernous chamber each member was recognized as "the Senator from Alabama, the Senator from Texas, the Senator from Kentucky etc." The Constitution had created a legislative assembly which had to be continually aware of the needs of people in the various states. The President's messages on the problems of the nation were examined in the light of those needs.

It seemed to me appropriate that all sessions of the Senate were opened with a prayer, presented by the clergyman who was designated as the chaplain. While the chaplain implored Almighty God to pour divine wisdom upon the legislators, the Senators sat at their desks or sauntered into the huge room. I did not feel any surge of spiritual activity there, so I decided that the official prayer was a rather empty ritual without any apparent effects upon the old men who had the responsibility of making laws for a confused and divided nation.

I often prepared an initial statement for Senator Scott Lucas, the first Majority Leader I served. I sat beside him with information about bills that would be proposed or debated, bills that had come to him with recommendations from the standing committees.

Frequently I brought mail and petitions to his attention while various Senators were making speeches. As the Majority Leader, Lucas was bombarded by arguments and appeals of all kinds. Month after month, he received forty to fifty thousand letters! Naturally, he couldn't read them all; he looked at summaries produced by his staff. When a letter came from a well-known person or was related to an urgent problem in his home state of Illinois, he would give it some thought. In many cases, he asked me to draft replies for his signature.

Charlie Murphy, David Lloyd, and other members of the White House staff telephoned me frequently, pushing me to get Lucas to be more active in gathering support for the President's measures. I made notes on what they wanted, and talked with him about their requests. He realized I still considered myself to be on Truman's team, and reminded me, "Kelly, we're trying to do the best we can for the President. But this is the Senate, not the White House. They've got to understand what we're up against." When I attended meetings of the Majority Policy Committee, I noted that Lucas couldn't get anything approved without the backing of the old men from the South. Sometimes it seemed to me that the South had really won the Civil War.

Lucas also had to deal with Kenneth Wherry, the Republican minority leader, who had a part in shaping legislation. Relations between the two leaders were often strained. When they stopped speaking directly to one another I had to stand in the middle of the main aisle of the Senate, relaying questions and statements back and forth between them—although the desks of the two men were only a few feet apart.

Occasionally, Wherry poked me in the ribs. "Tell your boss we want to get some action on that tax bill today," Wherry would shout. "Tell him to stop acting like a damned mule." Lucas heard him, of course, but Lucas spoke to me, "Tell the merry mortician I'm not gonna do it." Wherry would then get red with anger. He was an undertaker from Nebraska and he did not like to be described as a "merry mortician."

The behavior of Lucas and Wherry was one of the factors that convinced me the United States Senate was a peculiar place. When I began my service on Capitol Hill, a staff man with a weary face took me aside and described the situation as he saw it, "You're in a zoo with no cages, Kelly. Treat these old guys as you would lions and tigers roaming around lose. They are easily disturbed. Some of them have long fangs and short tempers. If you get in their way, you'll get bitten." I thanked him, and resolved to be as discreet as I could be.

On the floor, in the public debates on controversial issues, senators referred to one another with elaborate courtesy as "my distinguished colleague" or "My honorable friend." The same lawmakers would often plot in their hideaway offices to defeat bills by subtle maneuvers and then describe their opponents as "tricky" or "corrupt" or as "dirty fighters." Some of them went to great lengths to block any legislation that might go against the interests of their financial supporters.

Truman's hard-hitting campaign had angered some of the most powerful Republicans—particularly Robert Taft and Ken Wherry and others who felt he had used the Congress as a punching bag. It was almost impossible to get them to see the merits of Truman's proposals on domestic questions.

Perhaps the most significant event in the world in 1949 was the victory of the Chinese communists led by Mao Tse-tung over the nationalist forces of General Chiang Kai-shek. Although Truman was strongly opposed to communism, he felt that aid given to Chiang was largely wasted. He told David Lilienthal in May 1949 that Chiang's group was full of "grafters and crooks" who had stolen a billion dollars from funds intended to help the nationalist troops. In August, he released a "White Paper" containing severe criticisms of Chiang's government.

When Chiang and his officers had to flee to Taiwan, right-wing Republicans in the Senate contended that Truman did not understand the dangers involved in the rise of Mao, who had been regarded as "an agrarian reformer." The Republicans declared that Truman had "lost China."

Truman didn't believe China had ever been a possession of the United States. In November 1945 he had sent General George Marshall to China to advocate the formation of a coalition government that might replace the dictatorship of Chiang Kai-shek. His policy had been endorsed by the leaders of Britain and the Soviet Union. In February

1946, Marshall announced that an agreement had been reached by Chinese leaders to create such a government. But the refusal of Chiang Kai-shek to admit Communists into the proposed regime led to a breakdown in negotiations. A few months later Marshall returned to China to make another attempt to help the Chinese to form a united and democratic administration.

In August 1946 Marshall asserted publicly that an agreement could not be reached. In January 1947, he denounced the "dominant group of reactionaries" who had made it impossible to establish a genuine coalition. He also attacked the propaganda of the Chinese Communists, who created an atmosphere of continuing hostility. After Marshall returned to the United States, Truman dissolved the special agencies striving to help the Chinese move toward democracy, and he withdrew all American troops from China. The forces led by Mao Tse-tung then subjected the nationalists to a series of defeats, culminating in the withdrawal of Chiang Kai-shek and his followers from the mainland.

I was disgusted by the bitter statements of the Republican senators, who seemed to believe that Truman and Marshall could have prevented the revolution in China. I was disappointed by the attitudes of some of the Democratic members, who did not defend Marshall and Truman as vigorously as they should have. Senator Lucas was wary of the whole controversy, knowing that the *Chicago Tribune* and other reactionary papers in Illinois were putting Truman's policy toward China in the worst possible light.

I was increasingly disturbed by the lethargy of many of the Democrats in the Senate. Except for Brian McMahon of Connecticut, Hubert Humphrey of Minnesota, Herbert Lehman of New York, Paul Douglas of Illinois, and a few others, the Democrats often did not seem to recognize the necessity of standing by the President elected in 1948.

The White House staff was not able to mobilize public opinion for Truman's program. The Democratic National Committee tried to galvanize the labor unions, liberals, civil rights groups, and others who had helped Truman in his battle against the Republican 80th Congress. But the Committee did not seem to be as effective as it had been in the 1948 campaign. The Research Division, which had produced a torrent of ideas for Truman, had been abolished. The Committee fell back into routine activities.

I had hoped the Congress would act swiftly on the fourth point made by the President in his inaugural address—his call for a "a bold new program for making the benefits of our scientific advances and industrial progress available for the improvement and growth of underdeveloped countries." But Truman made the mistake of placing the responsibility for the development of that "bold new program" into the hands of the cautious functionaries in the Department of State. George Elsey, Clark Clifford, and David Lloyd—who were enthusiastic about it—could not get the President to create a new agency to move it forward.

I could not fire up Senator Lucas to take the lead in drafting a bill that might stir the Congress. I wanted to see the United States offer technical assistance and knowledge as rapidly as possible to the poor nations. to wipe out diseases and develop higher standards of living. Through the Marshall Plan, we had brought Western Europe into a booming recovery. We might have brought great benefits to the impoverished countries by pushing forward with the "Point Four" program. But the momentum was lacking.

As the months passed, I began to think that the strenuous efforts we had poured into the Truman campaign had been wasted. The noble goals of the Truman presidency were rarely mentioned. I produced speeches for Lucas and he delivered them with apparent satisfaction, but those speeches had few effects upon the public or upon the members of the Senate. Truman's victory had led me to believe that the right words, appealing to the idealism of the American people, had the power to accomplish many things.

But I did not see many accomplishments in 1949, during my first year as a writer and advisor for the Majority Leader. Truman did gain strong support for the North Atlantic Treaty which linked the United States, Canada, and ten countries in Western Europe in an agreement to defend one another. The Treaty committed the United States to the first peacetime alliance in the nation's history. I recognized its importance, because I shared Truman's belief that such an alliance might have prevented both of the World Wars. But it did not relieve the misery of the poor countries or bring benefits to the hundreds of millions of suffering people who needed the assistance of the United States.

Truman's inaugural address had conveyed his concern for the whole human family. But he seemed to be concentrating his attention upon the western countries. He had proved in his 1948 speeches and actions that he was a man with a global vision. I had hoped he would lead the whole world into a new era of peace and plenty. I wanted him to act much more boldly than he seemed capable of doing in the first year of his term. I expected him to go far beyond Franklin Roosevelt, even though I had admired "F.D.R." as a great leader.

In the atmosphere of the Senate, I became more and more conscious of how difficult it was for any President to get the majorities he needed for high achievements. Most of the Senators were preoccupied with promoting their own projects and their own careers, and most of the staff members appeared to be willing to do anything necessary in the cut-throat world of politics. Senators who had to run for re-election considered every proposal in the light of its impacts on various groups of voters in their states. Each Senator had a tendency to feel that his continuance in office was essential for the survival of the country.

While I was wrestling with the ethical questions that arose many times in the Senate's work—and waking at night with questions about what I was supposed to be doing with my own life—I began to think I had made a horrible mistake in leaving Boston University. I had been too easily convinced that I could make an important contribution to the Truman administration. If I had stayed in Boston I would have been teaching fine young people and learning much from them. I would have been writing stories. I might have been engaged in another book. I wished I had not been persuaded by Alfred Vigderman that Senator Lucas really needed what I could give him.

In those months Vigderman clashed with Margaret McMahon, who had been the administrative assistant to Lucas for eight or ten years. Vigderman suddenly resigned from the Senator's staff, and abruptly urged me to do so. He said I could easily get another job in Washington. I did not want to break with him, but I was reluctant to follow his advice. Lucas made it clear he wanted me to stay on in the position I had. Vigderman finally moved from the Senate staff to the State Department, where he had a long career.

I called Louis Lyons at the Nieman Foundation in Boston. He had encouraged me to go to Washington. Lyons told me it would be a reckless act for me to abandon a significant job. He understood my frustration and my depression about the Truman program's fate in Senate, but he reprimanded me for my impatience. He spoke of Truman's persistence and courage, and urged me to emulate the President.

My wife was stunned when I told her what Vigderman had asked me to do. She thought he was making an unreasonable demand. She reminded me that I had to give some consideration to her needs and to those of our son, Terry. She felt another move would be damaging to her and painful for Terry, who was happy with the other children in the Virginia suburb where we had found a comfortable apartment.

David Lloyd told me bluntly that I would be foolish to follow Vigderman. Lloyd assured me I was providing essential assistance to the President as well as to the Majority Leader. He said he understood my feelings, but he tried to get me to understand that everyone in political life had to endure many trials and disappointments.

"We know there's a lot of heat on you," Lloyd said. "But you can take it, Frank. We have to take it in the White House, too. The President takes it, day after day. He says that if we can't stand the heat we should get out of the kitchen. But we stand it—and so does he."

Remembering my obligations to my family and to the President, I decided to stay with Lucas. I began to write a satirical novel about a congressional investigation, entitled "Peckaworthy's Probe," and through that story I relieved my irritation at the antics of members of Congress. I also increased the number of martinis I had each night before dinner. The martinis made me mellow and then surly and finally helped me to sleep.

After Vigderman had gone, however, I had more opportunities for direct discussions with Lucas. He enjoyed my company and laughed at my jokes, and I began to appreciate the difficulties he faced in trying to please the President and the members of the Senate. I began to lose some of my impatience and to think like a Senator. My friends noticed a change in me. David Lloyd chided me for beginning to speak in a sonorous Senatorial manner.

The Majority Leader at that time had a palatial suite of rooms in the Senate wing of the Capitol. The rooms had been lavishly furnished by the Republicans in the 80th Congress, when they believed they would be in power for a long time. Lucas liked the suite, because he could have some privacy there—away from the constituents who pursued him in the Senate Office Building.

There were two offices in it—a pleasant one for me, with a fine desk and a leather couch which was available as a resting place when the Senate had sessions that ran for many hours; and a spacious chamber in which Lucas could hold off-the-record meetings with other Senators and advisors. That room had a ceiling twenty feet high, a glittering crystal chandelier, couches covered with gold cloth, a clock from Tiffany on a marble shelf, and paintings of George Washington and Abraham Lincoln. It had once been used as a judicial chamber by the Supreme Court of the United States, in the early days of the American Republic.

As the year 1950 approached—a year in which Lucas had to fight for his seat in the Senate—Margaret McMahon insisted that the Senator had to spend most of his time in the Senate Office Building, carrying out his duties as the Senior Senator from the heavily populated state of Illinois. The Senator decided I should move into the magnificent room with the tall chandelier. A quiet young man named Dean Ruth was hired as my assistant and a pretty blonde girl named Dottie Baker, the wife of Bobby Baker (then the head of the Senate's pages), was employed as my personal secretary. I was notified that I would have to increase my hours on duty, to aid the Senator in preparing for his campaign.

For a few months I had the exhilarating sensation of being lifted up to a special place in the Washington scene. I was ensconced in an expensive swivel chair behind the immense desk which had been provided for the Majority Leader. I worked on his speeches at that desk. I prepared agendas for the Senate and statements for the press. Without expecting it, I was catapulted into a high perch in the Capitol of the United Sates—in the very center of the American empire!

When I grew tired of dealing with the stacks of documents which flowed over my desk, I rose to my feet and walked to an enormous window which overlooked one of the spacious porches of the Capitol. Sometimes I could see tourists in the Capitol Plaza—people gazing with awe at the immense building which housed the Senate and the House of Representatives. Those people came from many states and many nations to see the Capitol in which so many historic events had occurred.

I found that my majestic office had noticeable effects upon the men and women who entered it. FBI men who came to talk with me about the loyalty of men nominated by the President for federal appointments were extremely respectful. Reporters who came in to ask me about legislation assumed I must know the secrets of leading Senators, or possess a notable influence. I enjoyed the prestige they attributed to me.

Occasionally, however, I was jolted by intruders who treated me almost rudely. The door would be flung open, and a Representative or Senator would walk into the room with a flock of wide-eyed voters. One of them said sharply, "Right over there, where that young fella is sitting now, the Supreme Court once sat." I felt immediately I was not an adequate replacement for the venerable judges who had occupied that chamber long ago.

Periodically my chandelier was cleaned by four ladies, who came into the office with small stepladders. They mounted the ladders, took down the cut-glass segments of the chandelier, wiped them with pieces of soft white cloth, and put them back again. I smiled at them and they smiled at me, but we did not speak, except to say "Good morning!" or "Good afternoon!" I noted their presence and then resumed writing at my desk. I had my job to do and they had theirs. I grew accustomed to being in an office in which ladies came to polish pieces of a glittering chandelier. I knew I wasn't dreaming because the telephone kept ringing and Senator Lucas occasionally arrived to discuss a speech or a statement with me.

Soon after I had been placed in that office, Senator Lucas asked me to be with him at a private luncheon with Drew Pearson, the Washington columnist whose reports appeared in newspapers across the country. Pearson claimed to be "a liberal" but he had been sharply critical of Truman. He was feared by Senators and cabinet members, because he used his column to build up some people and tear down others.

"I want you to be right there during my whole conversation with Pearson," Lucas insisted. "I want you to be a witness to every word I say to him. Make notes, too, if you have to. He's a twister. I don't want to have him distorting what I say or misquoting me—especially about anything connected with Truman's program. If he does put out a false report, we'll nail him. I don't want him to make trouble for me or for the President."

My presence with Lucas at that luncheon apparently impressed Pearson. A few days later, one of his "investigative reporters"—Jack Anderson, who took over the column in later years—came to my office, asked my secretary to leave, and closed the door. Anderson walked over to the tall window and gazed through it.

"What's on your mind, Jack?" I inquired. I was a bit impatient, because he had interrupted the work I was doing on a speech Lucas was scheduled to deliver that afternoon. "Drew and I have been talking about you," Anderson answered, without turning to face me. "We've heard you are more than a ghost writer. You're an influential man. You attend meetings of the Majority Policy Committee. You're consulted by Brien McMahon and other key senators. We think you should get more recognition."

"I'm not looking for that," I said. "I like what I'm doing and I don't want to have you and Drew build me up. Thanks for thinking of me, but I'm supposed to stay behind the scenes, Jack. I'm comfortable with that."

Anderson turned. He came over to my desk. "We can give you the kind of status that will make you a fixture here," Anderson said. I smiled at him. "I can't be a fixture," I said. "I'll be here as long as Lucas wants me to be, I suppose. That's it."

"Lucas may lose his seat in the Senate," Anderson said. "Everett Dirksen is running against him, and Dirksen is a hell of a campaigner.

The polls show that Lucas is ahead now, but not by much. Dirksen is traveling around Illinois, telling people that Lucas is a puppet for Truman. Harry's popularity has dropped."

"Lucas isn't anybody's puppet," I snapped. "He tells the White House people what he thinks. Or he asks me to make it clear to them." Anderson stepped closer to me. "That's what we want to hear about," he said. "Drew and I like to do columns about what happens behind the closed doors. People want that inside information. They should have it, too. The people have a right to know everything you guys are doing up here." "We have a press conference after every meeting of the policy committee," I said.

Anderson laughed. "Sure, you do. You feed a lot of pap to the hacks from the news agencies and other correspondents who grab your hand-outs and run. But Pearson and I want more than that. We have people all over Capitol Hill who tell us things. We have some in the White House, too."

"Some people like to leak," I said. "I guess it makes them feel important." Anderson frowned. "People want information," he said. "Drew and I provide it. We'd like to have you join our group. If you tell us what happens in those policy committee sessions, it'll help Lucas, too. I'm sure you'll put him in a good light. We'll build you both up, Kelly. And if Lucas loses, some senator on that committee will ask you to work for him. Or you could open a public relations office and get plenty of clients."

"And what would that do for me?" I asked. Anderson tapped the desk. "You could be a top lobbyist. You know a lot of powerful Senators. You could get your clients in to talk with them. You could make a hundred thousand a year, or more. Much more."

"I didn't come to Washington to be a rich lobbyist," I said. "I came here to work for Truman." "You have to think of your own future, too," Anderson said. "Truman probably won't run again. You could be around this town for a long time. You could lobby for good causes."

I was silent for a minute. I knew that "leaking" was an industry in Washington. Senators leaked. Committee staff members leaked information about key provisions in bills that affected pressure groups. The

Defense Department leaked. All the federal agencies leaked. Sometimes the leakers were "whistle blowers" who sought to stop unethical or illegal behavior. Sometimes they were instructed by their bosses to leak—to send up "trial balloons" or test the atmosphere for new ideas. I realized leaks had positive values in some cases—giving people vital information about what was occurring in a vast government which was obsessed with secrecy.

Anderson interpreted my silence to mean that I was considering his proposition. He went on, "All you have to do, Frank, is to go to a public telephone after each policy committee meeting and call one of these numbers." He put a card on my desk. "The numbers are on the back of that card. And there's a post office box number on it. You can send copies of documents to that box."

I didn't express the feeling of revulsion that rose in me. I said, "I'll have to think it over, Jack. I've never done anything like that."

"People are entitled to know what goes on here," Anderson said. "Remember that."

After Anderson had gone, I finished the speech on which I had been working. I took it over to the Senate cloakroom and gave it to Lucas. He read it, nodding his head. Then I described the offer Anderson had made to me.

"I'm not going to do it, of course," I said. "He tried to convince me that it might help you in your campaign. But I just can't do it. I can't be an informer for anybody." Lucas put his large right hand on my shoulder. "You can't count on Pearson and Anderson to do much for you or for me," Lucas said. "They're looking after themselves. I'm glad you told me about this right away."

"Anderson claimed the people ought to know everything that happens in the policy committee meetings," I muttered. "I've been a newspaper man. I know how he feels. He wants the inside stuff." Lucas stared at me. "Do the people have to know about every half-baked idea we toss around, Frank? About every joke I tell? About every long-winded story Alben Barkley goes through? About every sniping remark a Senator makes about Harry Truman or somebody in his cabinet? About all the gossip we've heard about Estes Kefauver and his women?"

I remembered one session of the committee in which Vice President Barkley had advised Senator McKellar to quit having sex with girls before breakfast. "That'll kill you, man," Barkley had snorted. "That love-making in the morning will ruin you." McKellar, who was in his eighties, had protested: "Aw, Alben, I don't do that." The other Senators had snickered while McKellar had grown red in the face.

"Maybe the public doesn't need to hear all of Barkley's tales," I said. "But shouldn't people know about all the maneuvering, all the faking? Shouldn't they know about the deceptions and the hypocritical masks some of the members wear?"

Lucas flushed. "You've never run for an office, Kelly. When you have to go through that, you'll know that politicians need a little privacy, a little freedom from reporters—from everybody who pokes into their lives. Why should we have to stand around in our underwear while everybody examines us?"

"I'm never going to be a candidate," I said. I shuddered at the thought. I couldn't understand why men would spend so much time and energy in fighting for places in the Congress. I remembered the angry letters I had seen in the torrents of mail. Whatever a Senator or a Representative did often seemed wrong to many of his constituents. It seemed to me that being a legislator was a thankless task.

"You'd better call Anderson and tell him to find somebody else," Lucas said, as we walked together into the Senate chamber. "I'll wait until I hear from him," I answered.

A week later, Anderson telephoned me. "I'm sitting here with Drew," he said. "What have you got to tell us." "Thanks, but I can't accept your proposal," I said. "Tell Drew that I hope he'll understand that I can't do it."

"You're passing up a big opportunity," Anderson reminded me. "We don't offer a chance like that to many people."

"I guess I'm not eager to be famous," I said. "And there's no shortage of leakers here on the Hill. You'll get plenty of information from them. I've got a different kind of job. I wouldn't sleep well if I tried to serve two purposes." "If Lucas loses, you'll be sorry you didn't work with us,"

Anderson said. Then he hung up.

I believed that people had a right to know how major decisions were reached in Senate committees, but I didn't have a right to slip information secretly to a special columnist—with the understanding that I would become widely known and eventually wealthy as a lobbyist. I had not come to Washington to make money. Harry Truman had lived frugally on his senatorial salary and Truman never exploited his position for personal gain. Truman was an honest public servant, and I thought his ethical standards were the ones to follow.

My wife had never expressed any desire to have a mink coat or to become a member of a country club or to ride around in a Cadillac. She completely supported my decision to reject Anderson's offer. So did other Senate staff members who knew about it. Some of them warned me, however, that I might regret that decision. One man shook his head ruefully. He chided me, "The name of the game here is power, Kelly. Access to a columnist gives you clout, buddy. Unless you are going to be a priest or a monk, you've got to have power and money."

One of my friends said bluntly, "If Lucas gets whipped in the next election, you'll have to scramble for another job. You might not get one. There may be three or four Senators who'll be beaten, and their staff guys could be competing with you for places. You missed a chance to be built up, man. Why are you in Washington if you don't want to play the game? If you want to be pure and holy, get out of politics."

I didn't think of myself as "pure" or "holy" but it was hard for me to accept the fact that many of the men I knew on Capitol Hill were cynical. They regarded large numbers of their fellow citizens as "dumb slobs who don't vote wisely" or as "greedy bastards" demanding favors. Many Senators and staff members were preoccupied with raising funds for their next campaigns. They were obsessed with money.

Truman had been forced to beg for dollars to keep his campaign train running in 1948, but he hadn't abandoned his basic principles. He had been a member of the Pendergast organization in Kansas City—and Tom Pendergast had been sent to prison for corrupt activities, but no charges were made against Truman. Truman had been investigated for years by his enemies, but his record of honest behavior had carried him through all the challenges he had faced. In World War II, his Senate Committee had conducted full and fair hearings. He had exposed profiteers and saved billions of dollars for the taxpayers.

In May 1949, at a time when I was getting depressed by the situation in the Senate, I had an unexpected opportunity to talk with the President in the Oval Office. I was asked to do a chapter about Truman in a book sponsored by the Overseas Press Club—a volume entitled *Men Who Make Your World*. Through his press secretary, Charlie Ross, I obtained an appointment with him.

Truman received me genially, knowing I came to interview him as a friend, not simply as a journalist or as a Senate staff man. He discussed with me the major decisions he had made in the four years since he had become president in 1945. He had shaken the world by his decision to use atomic bombs to end the war with Japan. He had helped to launch the United Nations; he had initiated the Marshall Plan, which had revived the countries of Western Europe after World War II; he had extended American assistance to other countries; he had broken the Soviet blockade of Berlin by authorizing an airlift of supplies into the city.

The atmosphere on that bright morning in May of 1949 was utterly different from the ambiance in the White House in the spring of 1948, when I had joined his campaign group. In that time of testing, Truman was under fire from the press, the public, the Republicans in Congress, and leaders in his own party who wanted to push him aside for another leader. I remembered the predictions of victory he had voiced in that crucial spring. The man who greeted me on May 27, 1949, had the buoyancy and confidence of a President who had overcome all the odds against him.

"What were the hardest decisions you've had to make?" I asked him. "If you mean the most painful, it would be the dropping of those bombs on Japan," Truman said. "I felt I had to do what I did, but I knew that those things would kill a lot of people. The atomic bomb seemed to me the most terrible thing ever developed, but I was convinced we could end the war with it."

I saw the anguish in his face. He had released the consuming power of nuclear destruction on two cities. His name would be forever linked with that decision. I knew he had prayed about it, and he had consulted many advisors, but he had taken the final responsibility for an action that had opened a new era in history—the atomic age. He had not sought the Presidency, but the weight of that job had fallen upon him.

Then Truman made a reference to the aggressive American general who had been a ruthless fighter for the Union in the Civil War—William Tecumseh Sherman, who had cut a swath of destruction when he led Union troops in a march through Georgia in 1864. Truman knew much about that war—and other events in history.

"You remember that old General Sherman said that war is hell," the President said in a somber voice. "We were in hell in what was going on in the Far East when I entered the White House. We were burning up thousands of Japanese men, women, and children with our B-29 raids, throwing fire bombs on their cities, setting them on fire." Then Truman turned his head and sighed. "And you know, Frank, that those Japanese are just as human as you and I are. We were burning up a lot of human beings."

I recalled what General Sherman had said about war. But his soldiers had never wreaked anything like the havoc brought upon Japan by American bombers. *Life* had printed pictures of the carnage inflicted by 300 planes on Tokyo in a single night—when more than 100,000 Japanese had been roasted in a fiery furnace. The stench rose for miles into the air.

In a radio address in 1945, Truman had urged the residents of Japanese industrial cities to move out of the target zones to safer areas. In that broadcast, made after he had decided to use atomic weapons, he told the American people, "I realize the tragic significance of the atomic bomb. Its production and its use were not lightly undertaken by this government…. We have used it in order to shorten the agony of war…."

When I sat facing Truman in the Oval Office on that morning in May of 1949, I felt a deep sympathy for the man. I thought of the unprecedented situation into which he had been plunged by the death of Roosevelt in April of 1945. He had been a reluctant candidate for Vice

President. He had not been informed about the progress of the atom bomb project. He had to rely on advisors chosen by Roosevelt—men who persuaded him that Roosevelt had been prepared to use such bombs when the weapons became available. In the midst of the slaughter and savagery of the war, he felt compelled to take the agonizing step he believed that Roosevelt would have taken if he had lived.

I was sure his experience as a combat veteran was an element in his decision. In World War I, as an artillery captain, he had ordered the killing of German soldiers with the guns under his command—and he had been surrounded by exploding shells from the enemy batteries. He believed his life had been spared by Almighty God because he had a mission to perform for his country and for humanity. But he knew mortal combat was the most terrible situation in which a decent man could find himself—forced to kill or be killed.

"I know you wanted to stop the killings as rapidly as possible," I said, "and you did it." "Our air force could have burned up Japan from one end to the other," Truman said. 'I wanted to save as many lives as I could—Japanese lives as well as American lives."

Although Truman acknowledged the fact that the Japanese government had incurred the wrath of the United States when Japanese planes had bombed the American naval base at Pearl Harbor, he did not accept the idea that unlimited punishment had to be inflicted upon Japan. In a telegram to Truman after the atomic bombings, Senator Richard Russell of Georgia urged him to tear Japan apart. Truman had replied, "My object is to save as many American lives as possible, but I also have a human feeling for the women and children of Japan...."

I felt sure that Truman also had "a human feeling" for the Japanese soldiers who had been indoctrinated by fanatical officers and then marched into battles. He knew that the Japanese people had no role in authorizing the Japanese planes to blow up American vessels in Hawaii. Truman was concerned about all the members of "the human family."

When I talked with him that day, I also remembered he had authorized the program for Japan's reconstruction carried out by General Douglas MacArthur and the occupation forces after the war. A democratic constitution was created for Japan, and the people of that nation were given democratic institutions, replacing the absolute power which had been exercised by the Emperor and his advisors. Japan rose from the ashes of the war to become one of the most prosperous nations in the Far East.

Truman spoke with me about the other significant decisions he had made as President in his first four years. I made notes, and used the statements he gave me for a chapter in the Overseas Press Club book. I will review these statements later on in this volume.

When I returned to my office in the Capitol that day, I was exhilarated. My faith in Truman had been reaffirmed. I resolved to work harder to help him to achieve his noble goals.

Harry S. Truman taking the oath of office at the White Office on April 12, 1945, after the death of President Roosevelt. (Mrs. Truman and their daughter Margaret are standing at Truman's left.)

Courtesy: U.S. Army & Harry S. Truman Library.

Winston Churchill, Harry S. Truman, and Joseph Stalin during war-time
conference at Potsdam, Germany.

Courtesy: U.S. Army & Harry S. Truman Library.

President Harry S. Truman announces the surrender of Japan on August 14, 1945, in his office at the White House. Seated at the far left is Admiral William D. Leahy, Chief of Staff, to his left is Secretary of State James F. Byrnes. Standing are members of the Cabinet.

Courtesy: Harry S. Truman Library.

President Harry S. Truman in a parade in Kansas City, Missouri, in June 1947, on the occasion of a reunion of the 35th Division, Battery D, Truman's unit in World War I.

Courtesy: International News Service & Harry S. Truman Library.

Return of President Truman and Senator Alben Barkley to Washington D.C. after the presidential election, November 5, 1948. Barkley was elected as the new Vice President.

Courtesy: National Park Service & Harry S. Truman Library.

President Truman and Vice President Alben Barkley in a motorcade through Washington D.C. following presidential election in November 1948.

Courtesy: National Park Service & Harry S. Truman Library.

Representative Peter Mack, Jr. introduces President Truman to a group of children from the 21st Illinois District, guests of the Congressman in Washington D.C., on June 21, 1950.

Courtesy: Harry S. Truman Library.

President Truman receives a group of New York State Democratic officials and college students in his office at the White House in June 1950.

Courtesy: Harry S. Truman Library.

CHAPTER ELEVEN

FEAR STRIKES THE SENATE—THE RISE OF JOSEPH McCARTHY

ON THE AFTERNOON OF FEBRUARY 20, 1950, I learned that the United States Senate could be swept by a wave of fear and intimidated by a demagogue. Until that day, I did not realize how much hidden anxiety existed in the Senate—and how one man could arouse so much hysteria.

I was sitting beside Senator Lucas when Senator Joseph McCarthy asked for time to speak. His slurred voice rising and falling in a strange sing-song tone, McCarthy launched into a wild attack on the Truman administration, asserting that "Communists" known to the Secretary of State were shaping the foreign policy of America. I knew and admired the Secretary, Dean Acheson, and I immediately whispered to Lucas, urging him to challenge every accusation McCarthy made. "The man's half drunk," I said. "He's pouring out poison."

I looked up and saw reporters in the press gallery above us making notes. It was a quiet day and the newspapers were always hungry for sensational material. McCarthy had gained national attention with a speech in Wheeling, West Virginia, claiming that there were 205 subversive persons in the State Department. In his rambling remarks in the Senate, he declared that he would cite 81 "cases" of people with "Communist connections."

"He can't document those charges," I muttered to Lucas. "Nail him. You could stop him cold." Lucas shifted in his chair and then he snapped, "I'm not going to get into a spraying contest with a skunk."

Unfortunately, Lucas was extremely reluctant to get into an argument with any other Senator. He was basically a timid man, unwilling to get into a slugging match. He permitted McCarthy to go on and on, and then he finally realized he had to do something. He was the

Majority Leader, identified with Truman's program, and he had to stand up and try to halt the flow of McCarthy's venom.

Lucas rose to his feet. He reminded McCarthy that the Senator from Wisconsin had previously mentioned 205 persons—and in another speech, in Reno, he had referred to 57 cases. The numbers did not seem to hang together.

McCarthy shuffled the papers he had on his desk. "I do not believe I mentioned the figure 205," McCarthy mumbled. "I believe I said over 200." He did not explain how the figure had dropped to 57 in Reno. He declared that the 81 "cases" he had brought into the Senate included the 57 he had mentioned in Reno, plus 24 additional ones.

Lucas asked him what he meant by "cases." McCarthy did not attempt to answer. Scowling at the Majority Leader, McCarthy said: "I am only giving the Senate cases in which it is clear that there is a definite Communist connection." He did not clarify what he meant by "a definite Communist connection."

McCarthy contradicted himself a few minutes later, asserting that some of the cases did not actually refer to "Communists" and admitting that "some of these individuals are no longer with the State Department." He flipped through the piles of papers he had stacked on his own desk and the desk of a nearby Senator. Some of the papers fell to the floor and he did not bother to pick them up. When he came to what he called "Case 72," he turned his head around in a puzzled way.

"I do not confuse this man as being a Communist," McCarthy said. "This individual was highly recommended by several witnesses as a high type...." Lucas did not ask him what he meant by "a high type," or ask whether there were other "cases' in which McCarthy had been in a state of confusion.

I was deeply disturbed when Lucas permitted McCarthy to hold the floor for nearly six hours. McCarthy's wild accusations were aimed at the Truman administration. He paced back and forth behind his desk, his whining voice rising and falling. Lucas did interrupt him frequently, until McCarthy snarled that he would not respond to any more "silly questions" from the Majority Leader. Instead of reprimanding the demagogue,

Lucas sat down.

Senator Brien McMahon, who had been an assistant attorney general before his election to the Senate, rushed into the chamber and made thirty-four attempts to show the contradictions and inconsistencies in McCarthy's charges. McCarthy brushed McMahon off with contemptuous remarks and went on talking.

Just before midnight, Lucas called for an adjournment. The turbulent session was over, but the smearing of Truman's aides had been thoroughly done. The absurd statements of Joe McCarthy were transmitted across the country by the news agencies. The fires of McCarthyism—which burned up the reputations of many good men—had started a conflagration of suspicion which was beyond the power of the Senate to control.

The Washington correspondents of major newspapers and broadcasting companies had taken a vote on the qualities of Senators a few weeks before McCarthy's rampage occurred. McCarthy had been rated "the worst member of the Senate" because he was regarded as untrustworthy, ineffective, incompetent. In spite of that, the reporters gave coverage to his sensational charges—although he did not bring forward any credible evidence to support his mud-slinging.

Although the United States was clearly the strongest and most secure nation on earth, many Americans were gripped by a fear of "communism" to the point of hysteria. With the encouragement of Senator Robert Taft and other Republican leaders, McCarthy played upon that hysteria successfully.

I became aware of my own susceptibility to the "red scare" when a false report reached the Senate that the Soviets were launching a rocket attack on Washington. The report supposedly came from the Pentagon. Senators and staff members went solemnly down into a cavern underneath the Capitol until the word came that the attack was not under way. I never learned the origin of that rumor.

I felt another surge of hysteria when the Soviets shot down an American naval plane over the Baltic Sea in April 1950. The Soviets claimed the pilot was spying on their activities in that region. Senator Lucas was asked to make a statement to the press and the broadcasting networks. I wrote a stern speech for him, assailing the Soviets and calling the destruction of the plane "a barbaric act."

The Majority Leader delivered my statement with a feverish voice on one network. Then he was asked to make it again on an overseas broadcast. As he approached the studio, I whispered: "Take it easy, Senator; we don't want to start a war over this." Lucas turned and glared at me. "Damn it, Frank, you wrote it. You'd better tone it down." I took the script and removed some of the tough phrases I had put into it.

When I went home that night I took my wife into my arms and confessed: "I guess I almost started a war today, but I didn't have the nerve to do it." She was startled, but she didn't take me seriously. She knew that the Majority Leader of the United States Senate would deliver to the world almost any words I gave him for a speech. She knew as well as I did then that the whole Congress would have to vote on a declaration of war—and one speech by the Majority Leader wouldn't stampede a majority into such drastic action.

But the fear and hatred of the Soviets—fanned by Joe McCarthy and the men behind him—increased almost daily. The Republicans had developed a plan to depict the Truman administration as "soft on communism." Lucas was linked to Truman, and so he was an easy target.

Everett Dirksen, a demagogic former congressman, was an ambitious Republican who wanted to knock Lucas out of his Senate seat. Dirksen had already begun to travel around Illinois, accusing Lucas of being a puppet for Harry Truman and the "radicals' in the Democratic party. Dirksen knew that Lucas had come from a farming family in Illinois and had no connections with "communists," but Dirksen and his campaign managers also knew that many voters were swayed by nasty accusations and big lies.

Because of his growing concern about the possibility of being beaten by Dirksen in the election, Lucas did not have the courage to be a leader in the struggle against a bill sponsored by three of the most reactionary members of Congress in autumn 1950. Karl Mundt, Richard Nixon, and Patrick McCarran advocated a bill to outlaw the Communist Party and to construct concentration camps for the detention of persons engaged in "subversive activities." Lucas was confident, of course, that President Truman would veto that bill because it obviously violated the Constitution of the United States.

When the bill finally came up on the Senate floor, only seven Senators mustered enough nerve to vote against it—Frank Graham, Theodore Green, Estes Kefauver, Edward Leahy, Herbert Lehman, James Murray, and Glen Taylor. Senators who were generally regarded as brave "Liberals"—including the passionate fighter for civil rights, Hubert H. Humphrey, and Paul Douglas, the junior Senator from Illinois, voted for it. I was shocked and horrified when I watched Humphrey and Douglas betray the people who had elected them.

I realized that Mundt and Nixon and Pat McCarran were willing to trample on the constitution and the Bill of Rights, but I had been certain that Humphrey and others would see that passing a bill to create concentration caps made a mockery of the war against Hitlerism—a war in which some of my friends had died.

Senator Douglas wrote later in his memoirs: "For the next two nights I couldn't sleep, as I pictured the persecution of the innocent that might come at the hands of the new Subversive Activities Control Board, of a new reign of terror settling over the country...." When Truman vetoed the bill, the President denounced it in scorching terms, saying he considered it to be the worst threat against the civil liberties of the American people passed by the Senate in his time.

When the motion to override Truman's veto came up in the Senate, Douglas supported the President—but Majority Leader Lucas and other Democratic senators voted to override it. Hubert Humphrey redeemed himself in my eyes by deciding that Truman was right in condemning the measure. The vote went against the President, however. Fifty-seven Senators voted against him and only ten stood with him. Many of the provisions in the bill were later declared to be unconstitutional by the Supreme Court.

I went out to Illinois with Lucas to participate in his struggle for re-election but I had lost my enthusiasm for him. It seemed to me that he would do almost anything to keep his place in the Senate. His identity as a human being was apparently tied closely to the respect he received as "a Senator"—as a member of the highest legislative body in the nation.

I was amazed by the ignorance of the Illinois voters. They appeared to know very little about what went on in Congress. The *Chicago Tribune* and other newspapers had evidently convinced them that the "communists" were going to launch an onslaught against the United States. The role Lucas had played in the enactment of the Marshall Plan—which had blocked communism in Western Europe—was overlooked or forgotten. The fact that Lucas had been chosen to be the Senate's Majority Leader did not seem to have much of an impact upon many of them.

I discovered that Lucas liked to travel in a rather luxurious style. As the Senate leader, he had a limousine at his disposal in Washington. In the search for votes, we rode through the towns and cities of Illinois in an air-conditioned Cadillac driven by a quiet chauffeur. In order to keep in touch with the White House, we had a telephone in the car.

When we arrived at an auditorium or a pleasant park with a platform for speakers, Lucas was usually greeted by local Democratic leaders. I often went into the crowds and listened to what the people were saying. I heard them comment on how prosperous he looked, on the expensive tailor-made suits he wore, on the number of times he referred to his responsibilities in the Senate.

Lucas tried to convince his fellow citizens that his high status in the federal government enabled him to bring benefits to his home state. I thought that was a good argument for keeping him in the Senate. But I heard men muttering: "He doesn't get out here much, except when there's an election. He likes that fast life in Washington. He's not one of us any more." Occasionally I heard a voice saying: "Maybe he's soft on the Reds."

I was startled when several men asked Lucas why Truman hadn't kept the Russians from "stealing the secrets of the atomic bomb." They didn't seem to realize that the "secrets" were known to many scientists. They didn't know the Soviets had brilliant researchers and also had captured German physicists who had helped the Soviets to develop an atomic energy program.

The poisonous suspicions spread by Senator Joe McCarthy and the House Un-American Activities Committee had penetrated the minds of many people in Illinois. They asked why Secretary of State Acheson had not denounced one of his aides, Alger Hiss, who had been accused of being a spy. They looked skeptical when Lucas reminded them that Hiss was believed to be innocent by Acheson and others. They wanted "dangerous aliens" and "radicals" to be jailed or deported. They didn't seem to understand the principles of the American Bill of Rights, established by Thomas Jefferson and other founders of the United States.

There was one leader in Illinois who did speak boldly in the Jeffersonian style. That was Robert Hutchins, then the head of the University of Chicago, who had refused to dismiss any teachers on his faculty because of their ideas and associations. He told a state commission investigating "subversive activities" that "the policy of repression cannot be justly enforced." In the dark atmosphere of those days, Hutchins was a shining figure who gave me hope for the future of the American experiment. I did not encounter him in my travels with Senator Lucas. But a few years later I had an opportunity to serve with him in the struggle to preserve the Constitution from the onslaughts of McCarthy and others.

As we went through Illinois that autumn I became deeply disturbed by the critical comments aimed at Lucas. I began to fear that he might be defeated. Although he was not a very courageous legislator, he did support many of the proposals advocated by Harry Truman. I had listened to some of Everett Dirksen's windy speeches and I was sure that Dirksen would do all he could to hammer at Truman.

"Senator, I'm sure you deserve to have the comfort of this car," I said to Lucas one afternoon as we approached Peoria. "But people tell me we are living in a style that's too rich. Dirksen is going around the state in an old Chevrolet. Maybe we should rent a Ford and put on some old clothes. People think we are dudes." Lucas leaned back and laughed. "Nobody has talked like that to me," he said. "Frank, you've been listening to the wrong folks. People here in Illinois are prosperous, and they know what we've done for them. They expect their senior Senator to dress well and do well."

"Maybe they won't tell you what they really think," I said. "They tell me you've gone too far in the Washington fast life. They don't believe you're one of them any more." Lucas seized my right shoulder. His voice was angry. "Just because you worked for Harry Truman in '48 and you pulled off a victory doesn't mean you know everything. I won two elections to the Senate before you came down the road, Kelly."

"I know you did," I answered him. "I don't claim to be an expert. The Truman campaign was the first one I ever got into. I just want to help you." Lucas relaxed. 'You've turned out some damned good speeches and you get along well with the newspaper guys," he said. "You did get me into trouble with the American Legion but that's blown over."

I had written a speech for him to give to the American Legion Convention in Chicago. I had suggested he speak on "The Great American Military Heroes," and he liked that topic because it gave him a chance to wear the mantle of patriotism. In the speech I cited the bravery and wisdom of George Washington, U.S. Grant, and noted generals and admirals in other wars. He had been loudly applauded, but he had been denounced in an editorial in the *Chicago Tribune* as "Mr. Bubblehead" because he had not mentioned the name of General Douglas MacArthur. When he asked me why I had omitted MacArthur, I had snapped, "I guess I didn't think he was a hero." I hadn't reminded him he had read the speech without noticing that MacArthur wasn't cited.

"Mr. Bubblehead," Lucas said, chuckling. "That's what the *Tribune* called me after I gave that fine speech you wrote for me. You gave them a chance to call me a new name." "They've called you worse names," I muttered. "At least they didn't say you were a Red."

As the campaign went on, Lucas was attacked by the enemies of Truman and by those who believed it was important to bring down the Democratic Leader of the Senate. Senator McCarthy stormed through Illinois, falsely accusing Lucas of being linked to "the communists in our government." Dirksen, a master of deceptive oratory, mesmerized many audiences that were easily manipulated.

Many doctors and their associates were angry at Lucas because he had supported President Truman's proposal for a national system of health care. Members of the American Medical Association raised large amounts of money to aid Dirksen. Doctors passed out pamphlets which depicted the Truman plan as a step toward "socialized medicine"—and depicted Lucas as an enthusiastic advocate of that plan.

Lucas didn't get much help from Adlai Stevenson, the witty and charming man who had been elected governor of Illinois by a landslide in 1948. Stevenson seldom left the executive mansion in Springfield during the 1950 campaign. He did deliver one speech I drafted for him, in which he referred to Dirksen as "a Pecksniff from Pekin." (Pecksniff was an oily character in a novel by Charles dickens, and Dirksen came from an Illinois town named Pekin.) Dirksen was an unctuous speaker who was often called by his critics "the Wizard of Ooze."

In contrast to Stevenson, Paul Douglas poured his energies into the effort to keep Lucas in the Senate. Douglas rented a station wagon and went through the streets of Chicago, urging everybody to vote for Lucas. He also traveled to the southern section of the state, calling on every citizen to cast a ballot for the Majority Leader. He also tried to persuade Stevenson to become active in the last weeks of the campaign, but Stevenson remained passive. Evidently Stevenson had his own political future in mind: he told Douglas that he did not want to alienate the many Republicans who had favored him in 1948.

Although most of the people I encountered in Illinois were prosperous, many of them had fears about the future. When President Truman had ordered American troops into battle in June 1950 to help the South Koreans repel the invading forces from North Korea, most of the citizens had regarded his action as right and necessary. But when many Americans were killed or wounded in Korea, attitudes began to change. Although Republican leaders had endorsed Truman's decision in June, they began to refer to it as "Truman's war."

When the American forces fighting under the United Nations banner were driven into a pell-mell retreat, denunciations of Truman and Senator Lucas became increasingly bitter. The *Chicago Tribune* printed a front-page cartoon showing Lucas stabbing an American soldier in the back with a bloody bayonet, although Lucas had nothing to do with the events in Korea. The *Tribune* blasted Truman and Lucas almost every day.

One of the Democratic Senators who had clashed with Truman and Lucas—Estes Kefauver of Tennessee—had become the chairman of a special Senate committee investigating crime. He decided to hold public hearings in Chicago shortly before the election, although he knew the hearings would bring up reports of corruption in the city's Democratic machine and probably damage all Democratic candidates. The questionable activities of Dan Gilbert, the Democratic nominee for sheriff of Cook County, drew extensive coverage in the Chicago newspapers. Lucas had no connection with Gilbert, but he knew the exposure of such activities would disgust many voters—and many of them might not vote for *any* Democratic nominee.

I was depressed by the fact that one Democratic Senator was apparently willing to sabotage another Democrat. Lucas told me he believed Kefauver had chosen to conduct those hearings because Kefauver viewed Lucas as a possible rival for the Democratic nomination for President in 1952. Kefauver had presidential ambitions and wanted to knock Lucas out of his way.

As we rode from one town to another, Lucas also voiced his suspicions of Adlai Stevenson. He was convinced Stevenson was really eager to get the 1952 presidential nomination. To do that, Stevenson would have to obtain the backing of powerful people in Illinois—people who might regard Lucas as a presidential contender if he won the senatorial election by a large margin in 1950.

"You can see that Stevenson isn't doing much to stir up the voters for me," Lucas said. "And Kefauver is doing all he can to discourage the Democrats this year. Estes doesn't give a damn about the Democratic Party. He wants the spotlight on him—and on his crusade against corruption. In his own way, he's knocking Truman, too."

I realized that American politics was a jungle in which men felt compelled to destroy their competitors. I sensed Lucas was very lonely, and I tried to encourage him by telling him I didn't believe Dirksen could fool enough voters to win. I reminded him that the Democratic

Party had been split in 1948, but Truman had gone on to triumph. He did not seem to enjoy hearing about Truman's triumph. He wasn't another Truman, and he couldn't do what Truman had done.

Two or three days before the November election, he suddenly invited me to go with him to his home town in the southern part of Illinois. He said, "We'll do a little duck hunting." "I've never done any hunting," I muttered. "My grandfather accidentally hit my father with birdshot while they were hunting one time. My father told me to avoid hunting."

"Nobody's going to fill you with birdshot," Lucas said, laughing. "When you go with me, you'll find out why so many men enjoy it. You're a writer, Kelly. You'd better learn something about hunting. You'll never forget it."

So I found myself on Election Day 1950, shivering in the darkness before dawn, wearing a pair of heavy boots, standing in a marshy place, holding a shotgun, peering at the sky. Suddenly I heard the thrumming of many wings beating in the distance above me. Standing next to me, Lucas muttered, "Here they come, Kelly. There's a flock coming right over us. Shoot when I do, you'll get one."

The sky was getting rosy and the quivering of the wings above us grew loud. I pointed my gun at the stream of ducks but I didn't want to kill any of them. I heard Lucas firing.

A beautiful bird dropped near us. Bright red blood gushed from a torn breast. Its wings flapped frantically. I was sorry I was there, and yet there was a desperate glory about that dying bird. It had been soaring in the sky and it had been brought down to a violent death. I wanted to pick it up and hold it against me, to comfort it, to know what it was like to feel the departure of life. My knees shook. I couldn't move.

Lucas tossed it into a canvas bag. "Well, we got one," he said. "Have you ever had a roasted duck for dinner? It's a feast." The harsh light of a cold autumn morning expanded around us. The thrumming of wings receded in the sky. The ducks were heading south. Lucas gave me a quizzical glance. "I didn't hear you firing, Kelly." I wondered whether the bird's heart was still beating. But I couldn't touch that bag. "I just couldn't do it," I said.

Lucas turned toward me. "You were in the army, weren't you? Didn't you do any shooting?" "We had plenty of rifle practice," I answered. "But I couldn't hit anything." "And yet they sent you overseas?" Lucas demanded. "They did," I said. "When I got over there, they made me into an army correspondent. The other guys did the shooting. I just wrote about what they did."

I remembered the golden day when I had gone into Paris in August of 1944 as a member of a victorious Allied force. I was called a "liberator" by the French people I encountered there, but I had not taken a direct part in the defeat of the Germans. I had not killed any of them. That had been done by the combat troops of General Patton's Third Army. I rode into the city with them.

"You couldn't have killed a Nazi if you had to?" Lucas asked me, as we got into his car. "Maybe I could have done it if one of them jumped me," I said. "My father killed Germans in the first war. He had to do it. He was in the infantry. I never got into any hand-to-hand fights."

As we drove along, Lucas spoke softly: "You're not against hunters, are you?" "No," I said. "And you are a good shot, and you enjoy it. But I just didn't have the urge to do it."

We went to his house, changed our clothes, and waited for the arrival of our driver with the Cadillac we had used in the campaign. We stepped into that luxurious car in silence. We began the long drive toward the city of Chicago, where we would be while the votes were being counted.

"Have you got a statement ready?" Lucas said. "The newspaper people will expect me to make a statement, whether we win or lose." "I've drafted a victory statement," I assured him. "I'm not expecting us to lose."

In each town, we stopped for a few minutes in a restaurant, a coffee shop, or a bar. Lucas went around to the customers in those places, shaking hands, asking them to be sure to vote—and to vote for him. I watched the Majority Leader of the United States Senate, a man who ranked in Washington just behind the President and the Vice President, begging coffee drinkers and waitresses to cast their ballots for him.

Lucas was disturbed when we left one restaurant. "Some of them won't shake hands with me. What the hell is the matter with them? I've worked hard for those people. They don't seem to know it."

"Dirksen has tied you to Truman," I said. "The war in Korea is going badly. They blame Truman—and you for supporting Truman." As the Cadillac purred smoothly along the highway, Lucas turned toward me. "Did you really think Truman was going to win, two years ago? Did you honestly think he had a chance?"

I remembered how my wife and I had listened to the early returns on the radio in New York, wondering whether Dewey would overwhelm the President. When the announcers began to tell us Truman was doing better than anybody had expected, we began to dance and clap our hands.

"I'm afraid I was affected by the pundits," I said. "I thought the odds were against him. But he was behind in the polls. You're leading." "Not by much," Lucas said. "I've heard there's a swing toward Dirksen. He has been all over the state for two years, doing his smooth talk and tearing me down." "And Joe McCarthy has been telling people that you are a Red," I said.

"How the hell can anybody believe that?" Lucas snapped. "I grew up in Illinois. My father was a farmer. They should know damned well I'm not a Red." "McCarthy has been telling them that Harry Truman is surrounded by Reds," I said. "And you've been trying to get Truman's program through the Senate."

"I haven't gone for every proposal Truman sent up to us," Lucas reminded me. Then he added, "Maybe I should have been more independent. That health plan made the doctors furious." "You're the Majority Leader," I said. "You had to work with the President."

I wished he had fought harder for Truman's bills. But he had to try to placate his critics in Illinois. Truman had carried Illinois by a few thousand votes in 1948. And Truman's popularity had gone steadily down after that.

We came to a town. Lucas and I went into a coffee shop and he greeted the people there. No one refused to shake hands with him, but their responses seemed to be perfunctory. When we returned to the Cadillac, Lucas slumped down in the seat next to me. His face was weary and sad. He muttered, "They didn't turn away from me in there, but it didn't feel right. They were letting go of me."

"You can't judge people just by the way they shake hands," I said. "The polls show that you still have an edge over Dirksen." Lucas snorted. "You don't believe those damned polls, do you Kelly? I can tell what they feel when I take their hands. It's bad today. Something's wrong. I'm afraid they're going to throw me out."

I remembered that Truman had declared that the shaking of hands was one of the vital factors in an election. Truman could sense how people felt when he touched them.

Lucas closed his eyes and bowed his head. If the people rejected him, he wouldn't know where he belonged. He was a Senator. That was his identity. If he didn't have that, he wouldn't know what to do. I thought he was going to weep, but he didn't.

As we rode on toward Chicago, I tried to comfort him, "Maybe the Cook County boys will turn out a big vote for you. They've claimed they can carry Chicago by a margin large enough to swing the state." I knew that Lucas, who had originally entered the Senate in 1938 with a victory as a New Deal reformer, had made an arm's length agreement with Jake Arvey and other leaders of the Cook County organization. With their support, he had been easily elected in 1944.

Lucas grunted. "The ward heelers in Chicago are going to try to save Sheriff Gilbert. I've heard the word that's going around in the Arvey machine—save the Sheriff and let Lucas go. I haven't played ball with Arvey." "That's a lousy thing to do," I said. "Why can't they go for you as well as the Sheriff?"

"The boys are trying to save their clout," Lucas said. "The Sheriff controls some jobs and they want to hang on to them. Kefauver came into Chicago primarily to beat me, but Gilbert got caught in Kefauver's meat grinder. He's one of their guys. I'm not. They'll put a lot into trying to save him, but not for me."

I thought of all the efforts we had employed to focus the public's attention on the legislative record Lucas had made during his twelve years in the Senate—and to show the contrast between his record and that compiled by Everett Dirksen during Dirksen's years in the House. But the election was not going to turn on what each man had done or failed to do. Joe McCarthy had poured poison into the voters' ears. Kefauver had done some damage.

During the early stages of that struggle in 1950, I thought that Senator Lucas might overcome all the obstacles he faced. But Lucas could not do what Truman had done in 1948. He was not equipped to go to the people week after week for face-to-face encounters. He was so steeped in the atmosphere of Washington that he was seldom able to talk in the terms that the citizens of Illinois wanted to hear.

If the United Nations forces in Korea—including the Americans fighting there because Truman had ordered them to keep the communists from conquering South Korea—had been on the verge of a sweeping triumph in November of 1950, a wave of exultation might have rolled through the United States that could have carried Lucas and other Democratic Senators back into office. But no triumph was in sight. Thousands of American lives were being lost. The Korean war seemed likely to go on for years.

On the election night, Lucas and I went to the suite of rooms in the Stevens Hotel where many of his friends had gathered. The trend against Lucas became evident soon after the polls closed. His days as a leader in Washington were being brought to an end by voters who had not realized how many things he had accomplished there.

Some of his friends began to leave the hotel suite at 9 o'clock, when a radio commentator predicted a landslide for Everett Dirksen. I heard one Democratic official say to his wife: "Let's get out of here. He can't do anything for us now." They hurried to the door.

Senator Paul Douglas rushed into the suite, brushing off the newspapermen who were beginning to assemble there. Lucas, Douglas, and I went into a small room to prepare a possible statement. I noticed that Lucas had tears in his eyes when Douglas put an arm around his shoulders. "I wanted to be with you, Scott," Douglas said softly. "It's a hard thing to accept. You deserved another term. Have you heard from Stevenson?" Lucas shook his head. "Not a word. I guess he doesn't want

157

to be with a loser."

I heard reporters shouting from the main room of the suite, yelling: "It's time to concede. Get Lucas out here!" Lucas flushed. "Hear that pack of wolves," he said. "I'm not going to talk to them. You handle them, Kelly."

The telephone rang. Lucas took the receiver and we heard a rapid voice speaking. When the voice paused, Lucas said, "That's it, then." He hung up and turned to us. "That was Jake Arvey. Enough votes have been counted in the key precincts to make it clear that I've lost. He wants me to congratulate Dirksen."

"Send him a telegram," Douglas said. Lucas nodded. "You write it, Kelly." He seized the telephone again and muttered, "Let me call my wife first. I don't want her to hear it on the radio." All through the campaign, his wife had stayed in their apartment in Washington. She couldn't stand the pain and strain of politics. Like Bess Truman, she preferred a quiet life.

I sat down at a desk in a corner and wrote a telegram addressed to Senator-Elect Dirksen. Suddenly I heard Lucas sobbing. In a broken voice he said, "Mama, you don't have a Senator any more. They beat me."

I remembered Truman had left his home in Independence on the election night in 1948—and had gone with a couple of Secret Service men to a place where reporters couldn't reach him. In spite of all his outward confidence, he might have felt that the voters had decided to evict him from the White House. No one could be sure of an election until the results were tallied.

"How's it going across the country?" I asked Douglas. The lines in his face deepened. "It's a bad night for Democrats," he said. "Then it's bad for Harry Truman," I said. Douglas nodded. "He's going to have a hard time with the next congress," Douglas said.

It struck me then that Truman's efforts to help the whole human family hadn't made the people realize that he needed the cooperation of the Congress to get his program going. I remembered the conversations I'd had with voters. Many of them seemed to swing from one opinion to another. Few of them had Truman's long-range vision.

I had to walk into the campaign suite and confront the mob of reporters and cameramen there. The glare of flashbulbs almost blinded me, but I was able to read the statement acknowledging the fact that Lucas had fallen. One reporter snapped at me, "Why doesn't he tell us how he feels about losing to Dirksen? What is he going to do now?" "He hasn't made any plans yet," I said. "He'll be in office until January. You'll have time to talk with him later."

Another question was thrown at me, "Do you think it was Joe McCarthy who did him in—or the Reds in Korea?" "You figure it out," I said. "You guys have the answers to everything."

The reporters finally left. I walked around the suite, trying to comfort some of the friends and relatives of Lucas, who were behaving like people at a funeral. I shared their grief. While I was aware of the Senator's faults and failures, I thought he had done enough to be re-elected. He had supported many of Truman's proposals. Dirksen would oppose them.

I talked briefly with Lucas and Paul Douglas. Lucas had the marks of tears on his face. He thanked me for all the work I had done and I told him I couldn't understand the behavior of the Illinois voters. Douglas shook hands with me, and I expressed my appreciation for the strenuous efforts he had made to help Lucas in the campaign. I wished that Adlai Stevenson had done as much.

But even if Stevenson had made speeches for Lucas from one end of Illinois to another, could Lucas still have run well against the stream of fear generated by Joe McCarthy and the *Chicago Tribune*? Could he have overcome the damage done by Estes Kefauver? Could he have convinced the Illinois voters that Lucas had nothing to do with the corruption in the Chicago organization?

I went to my room in the huge hotel and sat for a while with my head in my hands, wondering why I had plunged into politics. I went to the window and looked down upon the lights of the enormous city. Were people celebrating the Republican victory down there? Did they really believe that Scott Lucas, who put in so many long days in the Senate, trying to pass bills pushed by the President, had not been serving them as they wanted to be served?

I telephoned Barbara. I felt like weeping myself, but I didn't let the tears flow. Barbara had heard the announcement of the fall of the Majority Leader on a radio news broadcast. She had not been surprised, because she had felt the depression in my voice when I had called her earlier in the evening. "You did all you could," she said. "Other Democrats are losing. Tydings went down in Maryland. Nobody thought he could be beaten. It's a bad year. People are scared. They've lost confidence in Truman."

Truman had made the big decision to fight in Korea. After World War II, Americans were accustomed to triumphs. Yet our troops had been battered and driven back in Korea. The President was blamed.

After I had talked with Barbara I went to the window of the hotel room and stared down into the streets of Chicago. I thought of the people who were suffering and dying in that tough city. Women and children were being beaten there. Lucas and I were not the only men who were weeping that night. I thought I had shaken off the feelings of despair which had tormented me in my youth, but a surge of sorrow went through me.

Suddenly I remembered my conversation with Sister Mary Alcoque, the old nun I had visited in a convent a few miles from the hotel. She had been one of my teachers in Kansas City, and my mother had begged me to go see her.

As soon as I had entered her narrow room, I realized she was approaching death. I told her I was sorry to hear she had been ill. She gave me an examining glance. "I can see sadness in your face, Francis," she said, using my baptismal name. "It's you I'm concerned about. You've lost your faith in God and your religion." "I can't see God in this world," I answered. "There's so much pain; there is evil everywhere."

"God is everywhere, too," she said. "He overcomes all that." "I wish I could believe that," I muttered. "I have to be honest with you, Sister. I just can't believe it any more."

She had taken my hand. "Say one prayer with me, Francis. Say this prayer, right now. Oh Lord, forgive me for my unbelief."

"If I don't believe in God, how can I pray to Him?" I told her. "That doesn't make sense." "How do you know what makes sense?" she snapped back. "Do it for me. God knows you better than you do. Just recite it with me."

I went through the prayer with her, reluctantly and slowly. Then she released my hand and closed her eyes. I knew she would be departing soon. If anybody was in Heaven, she would be there. I hoped she would remember me.

As I stood in the hotel room that night, wounded by the downfall of Lucas, I wondered where I would go next. I had plunged into the world of politics with a winning President. But his victory had not enabled him to do many things he had promised to those who had supported him. With the crushing weight of that defeat in 1950 smashing me down, all the work I had done for Truman in 1948 seemed in vain. The people of my country didn't seem to know what they wanted.

I didn't feel the presence of God anywhere around me. Why had I recited that prayer in the convent to please an old nun? If a God existed, what would He think of a man who prayed to be forgiven for not believing in Him? Would such a God, the creator of all the worlds, the ruler of all the universes, pay any attention to a prayer like that? I had simply been childishly obedient to an old teacher who was obviously dying. I had been unable to refuse a request from a departing friend.

There was a bottle of bourbon whiskey on a tray in the hotel room. I knew Harry Truman liked that kind of whiskey. I drank a toast to Truman, and crawled into bed. I thought my time in politics was over. I didn't know that Truman had once declared in a letter to his wife; "We can never tell what is in store for us." I was exhausted and fell into a dreamless sleep.

CHAPTER TWELVE

STORMY YEARS AT HOME AND ABROAD—THE FINAL PHASE OF TRUMAN'S PRESIDENCY

WHEN LUCAS AND I RETURNED TO WASHINGTON after the November election, the specter of a possible war with China loomed on the horizon. Hundreds of thousands of Chinese troops were pouring into Korea. General MacArthur advocated the dropping of atomic bombs on Chinese cities. Prime Minister Attlee flew in from Britain, determined to persuade Truman to avoid a confrontation with China. Attlee and other European leaders had been alarmed by Truman's remark at a press conference that atomic weapons were available for possible use in the Korean war.

Truman assured Attlee that he did not intend to employ such weapons, but he refused Attlee's recommendation for negotiations with the Chinese at a time when Allied forces in Korea were being driven back. He also rejected a British proposal to give the Chinese government a membership in the United Nations. He told Attlee, "We will fight to the finish to stop this aggression."

A majority of Republicans in the House of Representatives blamed Dean Acheson, Truman's Secretary of State, for the losses suffered in Korea. They called for Acheson's removal, accusing him of being "soft on Communism." At a press conference, Truman declared, "No official in our government has been more alive to Communism's threat to freedom or more forceful in resisting it…." He expressed complete confidence in Acheson.

On December 13, Truman invited Congressional leaders to the White House. There he gave them a full review of the dangers to American security—based on CIA reports—and then called upon General George Marshall, his Secretary of Defense, who reported that the American army had halted the Chinese advance and would soon be able to regain the Korean territory that had been overrun. The atmosphere on Capitol Hill improved after that gathering.

Two days later, Truman spoke to the nation in a speech broadcast by radio and television stations. He acknowledged the existence of a crisis in Korea and called upon his fellow citizens to join him in a massive effort to overcome it. As he had done on other occasions, he evoked a strong response from the people.

"All of us will have to pay more taxes and do without things we like," Truman said. "Think of this, not as a sacrifice, but as an opportunity, an opportunity to defend the best kind of life that men have ever devised on this earth."

Although the 1950 election had brought defeat to some of his friends in the Senate and had brought harsh criticisms upon him, Truman continued to assert his leadership in international affairs. By the middle of January 1951, it was evident that the Chinese drive in Korea had collapsed. The American Eighth Army broke through the Chinese lines and American planes inflicted heavy casualties on the retreating Chinese. At the end of March, the Allied forces under the UN banner had recaptured Seoul, the capital of South Korea.

While the military situation improved immensely, Truman still had to deal with the eccentric behavior of General MacArthur. MacArthur was enraged by the decision to have the Eighth Army halt at the 38th Parallel—the boundary between South and North Korea. In an interview with Hugh Baillie, president of the United Press, MacArthur publicly questioned Truman's policy. MacArthur reminded Baillie that the UN forces operated under a UN resolution which called for "the unification of Korea." But Truman was angered by the General's statement, made at a time when the President was trying to deal realistically with the Chinese entry into the war.

Truman was engulfed in another controversy in Washington—a controversy which began when he announced that he wanted to add four more American divisions to the NATO army, to strengthen the defenses of Western Europe against a possible Soviet attack. General

Eisenhower, then the NATO commander, said the divisions were certainly needed.

Senator Wherry—the Republican leader who had clashed so often with Lucas—submitted a resolution demanding that the President had to get an authorization from Congress before he could dispatch troops. Truman insisted that he had the constitutional authority to send the divisions to Europe, but he wanted the Congress to indicate its support for the action he planned to take.

Hearings were held, and various members of Congress testified in favor of Truman's policy. One of them was a skinny young man from Massachusetts named John Kennedy, who spoke swiftly and eloquently. As I watched Kennedy, I thought he didn't look very strong or healthy. I couldn't imagine he would eventually reach the presidency; he didn't look well.

After a heated debate, the Senate agreed that Truman could order the divisions sent overseas under the North Atlantic Treaty but proclaimed that "no more could be sent without further Congressional approval." Senator Ernest McFarland, the amiable rancher from Arizona who had been elected the Majority Leader after the departure of Lucas, backed the President vigorously. Yet it was quite clear that the dominant member on the Democratic side in the Senate was Richard Russell, the chairman of the armed services committee. McFarland consulted Russell on every step he took.

I continued to serve as one of McFarland's assistants, although he had asked me to leave the palatial office I had occupied in the Capitol, because he wanted to use it himself. He assigned me to a desk in the Majority Policy Committee, which he also headed. He had appointed a man named Edward Cooper as the staff director of that committee, but he told me I would have direct access to him. He said it would take him two or three months to decide on the structure of his staff, but he hoped I would stay with him, perhaps as his principal speech writer.

I was impressed by Truman's steady strength in one crisis after another, and I was tempted to think that I might continue to help the President by sticking with the new Majority Leader. David Lloyd and other friends on the White House staff urged me to stay in that job as long as I could.

While Harry Truman was struggling to prevent a widening of the war in Asia, I was going through a personal turmoil. After the election I had been offered an appointment as an aide to Averell Harriman, who was then the director of the Mutual Security Administration and one of Truman's closest advisors. I was told that Harriman might seek the Democratic nomination for president in 1952. I was doubtful about getting into another political campaign—one perhaps more strenuous than the ones I had gone through in 1948 and 1950.

My novel, *An Edge of Light*, had not been a best seller but it had received good reviews in publications across the country. The Atlantic Monthly Press editors thought it was time for me to produce another book. I began to outline a satire on a Congressional investigation, tentatively entitled *Peckaworthy's Probe*. I used my knowledge of Congressional capers to express my feelings about the eccentric behavior of members of Congress who frustrated the President and blocked progress.

Day after day I went to my job in the Senate, drafting statements for McFarland, trying to persuade him to be more aggressive in getting Truman's proposals out of Senate committees. He was an easy-going man, not as ambitious as Lucas had been. He liked what I wrote for him but he couldn't deliver speeches with much passion. He said to me, "I wish I could be an orator like Winston Churchill, but I'm not. I just can't talk like that."

Relations between Truman and General MacArthur grew worse and worse. Without consulting the President, MacArthur issued statements declaring he knew how to win the war in Korea—and plainly indicating he didn't think Truman's policies could be successful. Truman summoned McFarland and other Congressional leaders to the White House to tell them that the Joint Chiefs of Staff were advising him to remove General MacArthur.

"There's going to be a hell of a fight," McFarland told me when he returned from one of those meetings. "MacArthur's a hero to a lot of people in Arizona and all the other states, I guess. There'll be a terrible uproar." "But you'll back the President," I said. "There'll be cries for his impeachment." McFarland sighed. "Yes, I'll back him," he said. "It may cost me my seat in the Senate, but I'll do it. We can't have a general telling off the President."

Charlie Murphy, Truman's counselor, had invited members of the Senate staff to a session after Truman had made it known he intended to fire MacArthur. We were asked to give our opinions on how much support Truman would receive in the Senate—and how severe the public reaction would be. All of us agreed that it would be "a firestorm" but no one disputed the decision. All of us knew how arrogant MacArthur had been, and all of us admired the immense patience Truman had shown in dealing with him.

On April 11, 1951, Truman announced that he had relieved MacArthur of his military commands in the Far East. The President said, "With deep regret, I have concluded that General of the Army Douglas MacArthur is unable to give his wholehearted support to the policies of the United States government and of the United Nations in matters pertaining to his official duties. In view of the specific responsibilities imposed upon me by the Constitution of the United States and the added responsibility which has been entrusted to me by the United Nations, I have decided that I must make a change of command in the Far East...." He appointed General Matthew Ridgway as MacArthur's successor.

On the morning after Truman made that announcement, I went to the Senate Office Building for a meeting with Senator McFarland. I saw bags of mail and stacks of telegrams in the hallway and in McFarland's offices. I opened some of the telegrams and I was shocked by the messages. Some of them ordered McFarland and other Senators to go immediately to the White House and drag President Truman out of his office, perhaps to be hanged on the nearest lamp post. Others demanded that Truman should be put on trial for dishonorable actions—and impeached as soon as possible.

Richard Nixon, who had moved from the House to the Senate by making wild charges in the 1950 campaign with the support of Joe McCarthy, joined in the attacks on Truman. Senator William Jenner of

Indiana, shouting and spitting on the Senate floor, yelled, "I charge that this country today is in the hands of a secret inner coterie which is directed by agents of the Soviet Union. Our only choice is to impeach President Truman." Effigies of Truman and Acheson were burned by angry citizens in town squares and on college campuses.

Representative Joseph Martin, the Republican leader in the House of Representatives, invited General MacArthur to return to Washington at once—to speak to a joint session of Congress. Martin and MacArthur had been exchanging letters, and Martin felt that the general had a right to express his views to the nation.

Although he felt his action in removing MacArthur was justified, President Truman continued to voice admiration for MacArthur's genius and for the general's achievements in administering Japan during the period of Allied occupation. MacArthur had helped the Japanese to create a democratic constitution and to build a new political system. Truman declared that it was proper for MacArthur to address the Congress.

MacArthur received a tremendous welcome in San Francisco when he landed there, with hundreds of thousands of citizens cheering him in the streets. He was also hailed as a hero when he came up to Capitol Hill. With other Senate staff members, I stood in the House chamber when he entered it amid thunderous outbursts of applause.

At the end of his emotional speech—in which he claimed he could have won the war in Korea—MacArthur announced he was finishing his military career and that he would "just fade away, an old soldier who tried to do his duty as God gave him the light to see that duty." I looked around me and saw tears running down the faces of Senators and Representatives. I didn't shed any tears myself. I was deeply relieved, because I feared that MacArthur might call upon the Congress to drive Truman from the White House.

President Truman had read many volumes of American history. He knew the American people were often aroused to high stages of feeling but were not likely to support any military leader who threatened to overthrow their government. He was sure that MacArthur was well aware of the constitutional authority of a President. In fact, MacArthur would probably seek the Oval Office in the election of 1952.

When a Senate committee, chaired by Richard Russell, obtained the testimony of the Joint Chiefs of Staff, it became evident that MacArthur did not have the backing of his fellow officers. General Omar Bradley said that MacArthur's proposals for bombing Manchuria and hitting China "would involve us in the wrong war, at the wrong place, at the wrong time...." General Vandenberg, the chief of the air force, asserted that an aerial assault on Manchuria might cause losses that would cripple the air force for years. Admiral Sherman scoffed at MacArthur's idea for a naval blockade of China. MacArthur himself finally acknowledged it would be insane to plunge into Manchuria and become involved in a long war with China.

My admiration for Truman's calm handling of the MacArthur controversy led me to decide that I should remain on McFarland's staff, doing what I could to secure the adoption of some of the President's recommendations. McFarland was a quiet, cautious man who liked to work behind the scenes. He knew he would face a hard fight for re-election in Arizona. He had heard that the Republicans were going to nominate a man who was an excellent speaker and had many friends—a man named Barry Goldwater. Arizona was a conservative state and the Truman program was not very popular there.

When I had examined the mail and telegrams sent to McFarland after the removal of MacArthur, I had realized what McFarland was up against. MacArthur had many admirers there, and their anger against the Truman administration led them to swing heavily to the Republican side. Goldwater appealed to the right-wing groups which opposed almost everything Truman favored.

Although I got along well with McFarland, I became deeply depressed by the atmosphere in the Senate. The rampages of Joe McCarthy became worse and worse, and few Senators stood up against him. McCarthy hurled epithets at Truman and tried to smash the reputations of Truman's staff members. I tried to persuade McFarland to organize a group of Senators to oppose him, but McFarland rejected the idea.

At my wife's urging, I consulted a physician—a psychiatrist named

Julius Schreiber, a calm doctor with a kindly face and a hearty laugh. When I told him I would be embarrassed if any of my friends knew I was seeing a psychiatrist, Dr. Schreiber answered, "You'd be surprised to know how many well-known politicians have cried on my couch. Washington is a hard place, a place full of pain. There are many people in anguish here. Some of them are on the verge of suicide. Others collapse or take their lives."

When I admitted to him I didn't know what I was going to do next—and I didn't feel able to cope with any more crises—he comforted me by saying, "You're living in a maelstrom. Truman can stand it, because he won his last battle. He has people around him who can sustain him. You do, too. You are stronger than you think you are. When you get better, you'll see new possibilities all around you."

"I'm on the road my father took," I said. I poured out the fears and fantasies of my childhood and youth. I described the love and rage that came to me from my memories of my father. I admitted I had become angry toward my wife—and I had been harsh and cruel to my small son. I told him I was tempted to take refuge in a liquor bottle, as my father had. "You're not your father," Schreiber growled. "You'll have a better life than he had."

I told him I wished I could be like Harry Truman. Truman seemed to have an unshakable faith, based on the God of the Bible. I had discarded my Catholic training, which had emphasized sins and the punishments God could inflict on sinners in a place called "purgatory" or "hell." But I had not been released from my feelings of guilt. I blamed myself for every failure.

"Truman told me he dropped the atom bombs on Japan to get us out of hell," I said. "He realized we were burning up thousand of men, women and children with fire bombs. He wanted to get the war over and stop that kind of hell. But you can't get out of hell with atom bombs. I don't know why Truman thought we could. What we did to those Japanese cities was a form of hell. Truman will always be connected with the pillars of smoke that went up from Hiroshima and Nagasaki. And I will always be connected with Truman."

Schreiber was not a detached, distant therapist—the sort of analyst who let people go on and on without intervening or giving advice. He snorted at me. "You let Truman carry his own load," Schreiber said. "I don't think he's as great as you think he is. But he's capable of carrying his own burden. You don't have to do it, just because you helped him to get elected in 1948. But you do have to get rid of all the fears you have about your sins. I'm sure you've got plenty of them. Yet you don't have to let your sins overwhelm you. You may discover a God who loves you, no matter what you've done."

Unlike many analysts, Schreiber did not show scorn for religion or regard it as an infantile delusion to be thrown off by a mature person. He helped me to realize that I had a persistent hunger for God, for a divine power in my life. He said I didn't have to return to the Roman Catholic church, but it might be healthy for me to pray, to acknowledge my dependence upon the Mighty Power which shaped the universe.

I mentioned to him the absurd prayer I had recited with the old nun in her hospital room. I muttered, "That was crazy." "No, it wasn't," Schreiber said. "She offered you a chance to acknowledge a power greater than yourself. That prayer may be one of the factors that brought you here."

Schreiber wasn't a formally religious man. But he knew that strange things happened in the course of meetings—things he couldn't explain in terms of Freud and Jung and other physicians of the mind. He shared Einstein's view that there was a Spirit in the universe far beyond human comprehension.

With Dr. Schreiber's healing presence, I was released from many of my anxieties. I cut down on the number of martinis I drank. I gave more tenderness to my wife and my son. I realized I had a brilliant child and spent much time with him. Barbara was aware of my desire to have our marriage endure. Our union in love meant more to me than anything else on earth. She forgave me when I sank occasionally into depression and rage. I recovered more quickly than I had done before.

McFarland asked me to be with him on the Senate floor. I felt my position with him was fairly secure. I tried to write speeches in the plain style he liked. He expressed his appreciation for what I did and invited me to attend meetings of the Majority Policy Committee.

Then I had a pleading call from the White House—a request from David Lloyd, who said he had been informed that Senator McCarthy was going to make an attack on him at the next session of the Senate. He had become one of Truman's most active assistants, and McCarthy had been given information about him that could be used against him and might damage the President.

As a young attorney, Lloyd had been a member of the National Lawyers Guild, which had been labeled as a "left-wing group." Lloyd was no longer a member of it, but he had heard that McCarthy intended to claim he was "a dangerous subversive" who should be ejected from the President's staff.

"The President won't pay any attention to what McCarthy says," I assured him. "You know that." "But I'd like to have somebody stand up in the Senate and face him down," Lloyd said. "Will you ask Senator McFarland to speak for me? I'll send you a prepared statement." "I'll ask him," I said. "He doesn't like to tangle with McCarthy. Who does? I'll certainly express my own respect for you."

When I urged McFarland to defend Lloyd, his ruddy face hardened. "I can't do it, Frank. You know I'm going to have a tough fight next year. McCarthy will come to Arizona and speak for Goldwater. I don't want McCarthy going after me."

"Dave Lloyd worked with me on Truman's campaign staff," I said. "He isn't a Red. McCarthy won't get anywhere by trying to smear him. He's a fine man." McFarland rubbed his jaw. "If you say so, I'm sure he is. Then let Harry Truman defend him. I'll stand up for anybody on my own staff. He's the President's man. Harry can take care of him."

I realized again that the defeats of Scott Lucas and Millard Tydings, two noted Senators, had made other members of the Senate fearful of McCarthy's venom. The miasma of McCarthyism was spreading through the country. I couldn't argue with McFarland.

When the statement about Lloyd came to me from the White House, I decided to try to find a senator who wasn't running for re-election. In the Senate cloakroom I encountered Hubert Humphrey, who had become a friend of mine. Humphrey was admired and liked by everybody in the Senate. I went over to him and showed him the statement I had received. "McCarthy's going to jump on Dave Lloyd?" Humphrey exclaimed. "McCarthy should be ashamed of himself. Give me that statement. I'll speak up for Lloyd."

Humphrey did what he had promised to do. He confronted McCarthy on the floor of the Senate and McCarthy backed away from Lloyd's case. When McCarthy was challenged, he often dropped one accusation and rambled on to another. He didn't like to face Humphrey, who was not afraid of him.

I was depressed by McFarland's attitude toward the President. I began to think I should have accepted an offer to take another job. A few days later, McFarland disturbed me by saying that a capable young writer from Arizona might join his staff. He said he had heard that I had rejected offers of positions with a higher salary than I was getting from the Senate. He told me he wanted me to be free to go elsewhere if I wanted to do so.

Shaken by that conversation, I went down to the dining room in the Senate wing of the Capitol, ordered some coffee and a bowl of bean soup, and sat there staring into space. Bill White, a Washington correspondent for the *New York Times*, came over and sat down near me. I had arranged interviews with Lucas for White, and we got along well. "How's McFarland these days?" White asked. "He's not a very active leader, is he? I hope you can pump some life into him. He needs help."

"He doesn't seem to think he needs help from me," I said. "He's encouraging me to take another job." "What?" White swung toward me. "He'll have to be straightened out. I'm going to talk with Lyndon about this. McFarland needs a guy with your brains and experience, Frank."

White came from Texas. He was reported to be a close friend of a new member of the Senate—Lyndon Johnson, who had been ironically called "Landslide Lyndon," because he had won a primary runoff election by just 87 votes and the legality of those votes had been questioned.

"What can Lyndon do about it?" I asked. "He can talk to Dick

Russell," White said. "Russell knows about your work. McFarland listens to Russell—and he pays attention to Lyndon, too."

Johnson had already become known as an arm-twister—an aggressive man who threw his weight around. After two years in the Senate, Johnson had established himself as a member of Russell's inner circle.

"I doubt that Johnson will get into this," I said. "He has plenty of other things to do." "He will if I ask him," White said. "You're going to stay with McFarland, Frank. Lyndon will see to that."

Like Johnson, Bill White was decisive. He thought he knew what was best for me—and for the Majority Leader, too. His articles in the *Times* about the Senate were widely read. He could build a Senator up, or tear one down.

As White strode from the Senate dining room, I felt uneasy. If Johnson forced McFarland to retain me, I might not have a friendly relationship with him. In spite of White's assurance, I doubted that Johnson would attempt to tell McFarland what to do about a staff member. I didn't know then how arrogant Lyndon Johnson could be.

When I went home that night, I shared my concerns with Barbara. She suggested I might seek the advice of Louis Lyons, the curator of the Nieman Foundation at Harvard, who had recommended me for several positions. Lyons informed me that Dr. James Conant, then the president of Harvard, was involved in the creation of a new organization to be entitled "The Committee on the Present Danger," which would attempt to awaken citizens to the perils of the nuclear age through educational programs. Tracy Voorhees, a former Secretary of the Army, was forming the group and was hunting for a staff director who would have an office in Washington. Lyons said he would ask Voorhees to call me.

The next day, Voorhees and I had a productive meeting. The Committee had developed comprehensive plans for obtaining coverage in the mass media. I was informed that President Truman knew about the committee's formation and considered it important. Truman was deeply alarmed by the dangers of atomic weapons and wanted to have them placed under international control as soon as possible. The Committee wanted to have a Washington director who could work well with the White House and the Senate. Voorhees said he thought I had the qualifications they considered to be necessary.

Two days later, Voorhees telephoned me. He said that Dr. Conant and others on the Committee had approved my appointment. The compensation would be higher than the salary I received from the Senate. He asked me to find out from Senator McFarland the date when I could begin my new work.

When I talked with McFarland, he said that Voorhees had already informed him about the Committee's plans. He had known Voorhees for some years. He was impressed by the caliber of the Committee members and congratulated me on my opportunity to serve with them. He said I could leave by the end of the month.

When I left McFarland's office that day, I was exhilarated. Although I liked McFarland very much, I knew he could not be the effective leader who was needed to get Truman's program enacted. He couldn't break the stalemate in the Senate. I thought the Committee on the Present Danger might be able to have a strong impact on the public. With that Committee, I would be serving the cause of humanity.

My euphoria didn't last long. At the end of the week McFarland summoned me. When I came into his presence, his eyes indicated that he was disturbed but he treated me with his usual courtesy. "Lyndon Johnson has asked for a meeting this afternoon with us," McFarland said. "He's not happy about your decision to leave the Senate staff. We will meet with him at 3 o'clock. Dick Russell will join us."

I was astounded by that announcement. I knew Russell was an extremely busy man. In addition to being chairman of the Armed Services Committee, he was a senior member of other major committees. He had the admiration of Republicans as well as Democrats.

What happened at the session in McFarland's office that afternoon was a curious performance. I arrived a few minutes early. McFarland was alone, sitting in a black swivel chair with a high leather back. His feet were propped up on his desk, near a small statue of a cowboy on a bucking horse.

McFarland looked at me as if he had never seen me before. I saw in his eyes a mixture of respect, irritation and amazement. He put his feet down and rubbed his jaw thoughtfully. "You've made a big impression on that reporter, Bill White," McFarland muttered, after a moment. "He has been telling Lyndon that we ought to ask you to stay with us. He has persuaded Dick Russell to come to this meeting."

Senator Russell entered the office before I could comment. Russell shook hands with me warmly. He was smiling and friendly. I didn't agree with Russell's views on segregation and civil rights, but I thought he had done a superb job in handling the MacArthur controversy. He was interested in history and poetry, and we had enjoyed our conversations about books and writing.

Lyndon Johnson came in last, with a grim expression on his shrewd face. He was a huge man who radiated a sense of self-confidence and ambition. I had heard he would like to become the Majority Leader of the Senate if McFarland lost his contest with Barry Goldwater.

"Lyndon, you asked for this meeting," McFarland said with a slow drawl. "As we all know, Frank has been offered a job by Tracy Voorhees, to work with that new Committee headed by Dr. Conant. It pays more than we can pay him here, and I encouraged him to take it."

Russell said, "I'm not surprised they made you an offer, Frank. And I know Tracy, of course. He was a good Secretary of the Army. The members of that Committee are fine people. Lyndon, why do you think Frank should turn them down?"

Johnson stared at McFarland. "Mac, Bill White tells me that Frank Kelly has the experience and ability to be valuable to you and to the Senate. It's more important for him to stay here, serving his country, than to take that offer. The United States Senate is more important than any Committee headed by Dr. Conant or anybody else. You know that. We all know that."

Russell interrupted. "Lyndon, we can't keep Frank here if he thinks he has a better opportunity. We're all committed to being in the Senate; we think the Senate is the most important place in the world. But Frank hasn't necessarily dedicated his life to being with us. He has a right to go elsewhere, any time he decides to do that."

"I guess I gave Frank the notion that he should look around for another position," McFarland said. "I thought I'd bring in a man from Arizona." "That's the way it happened," I agreed, turning to Johnson. "Senator, I know the importance of being the assistant to the Majority Leader. I've been honored to work here. But I certainly realized that Senator McFarland could bring in another man if he wanted to do that."

Johnson looked at McFarland. "Mac, you made a mistake," he said bluntly. "Here's a man who worked two years for Scott Lucas when Lucas was our leader. Kelly knows the ropes. Bill White says he has friends in the White House and in the press gallery and all over the Hill. This man can be useful to you and to the Senate, and he should stay right here."

"Senator Johnson, I hope you understand how I feel," I said then.

Johnson roared, "How you feel is not the point here, Kelly. You want to know what I think of you? Here you are, the assistant to the Leader of the United States Senate, a Leader who ranks next to the President and the Vice President of our country. What you can do for Senator McFarland is valuable to this country and to the United States Senate, the highest legislative body in the world. I think he realizes now that you can be very helpful to him. You should be eager to stay with him."

"Senator, I gave my word to Tracy Voorhees that I would work for his organization," I said. "I had Senator McFarland's consent for that."

Johnson snorted, "Kelly, you'd better get things straight. I've pointed out to Mac that he needs you, and you should be proud of that. In your job, you are standing next to one of the leaders of this country. It's like you are right next to an admiral in command of our fleet. You couldn't grab the admiral by his sleeve and tell him you wanted to go ashore. You couldn't do that in the navy, and you can't do it here. It's your duty—get that straight. It's your duty to stay with the Majority Leader as long as he needs you. Get that straight."

I was astonished by Johnson's vehemence. He seemed to regard the Senate as a sacred institution to be venerated. He had fought hard to get his place in the Senate. He identified himself with it—and he identified the good of the nation with that institution.

"Lyndon, take it easy," McFarland said. "I encouraged Frank to do what he considered best for himself and his family. I can't order him to stay here."

Senator Russell turned to Johnson. He was frowning. "Cool off," Russell said. But Johnson went on, "Mac, you should call the Pentagon and have Kelly commissioned at whatever rank you want him to have— and have him assigned to your office. That's the way to handle it." Russell glanced at me, and snapped, "Lyndon, I'd never sanction any such thing. Frank, don't you worry. The Pentagon wouldn't move without consulting me."

Johnson moved toward the door. "We can't spend any more time on this. Mac, I've told you the right thing to do. Kelly, you think about what your duty is. You should stay here with Mac." McFarland rose from behind his desk. "Aw, Lyndon," he said, an uncertain smile on his face. "You're kiddin', Lyndon."

"The hell I am," Johnson said. He walked into the corridor and slammed the door behind him. There was a silence after Johnson's departure.

McFarland came over and put his right hand on my shoulder. "Lyndon was just kiddin', Frank," McFarland muttered. "Bill White must have pumped him up. He thinks a lot of you."

"I'm not in the army reserves," I said. "I don't think the Pentagon could pull me in legally." Russell whacked me on the back. "Lyndon thinks the Senate is the greatest place in the world," Russell said. "He gets mad at anybody who doesn't agree with him. That doesn't mean you have to stay with us. You're free to go."

I heard later Johnson was angered by a staff member who wanted to resign—and Johnson learned that the man was in the naval reserve. The man went back into uniform and found himself on duty in the Aleutian Islands.

Whether Johnson was kidding or not in my case—and Russell obviously didn't think he was—Johnson got his way. When I telephoned Tracy Voorhees to tell him about the meeting in McFarland's office, Voorhees said abruptly: "It's clear to me you should remain in your position with the Majority Leader, Frank. We'll have to withdraw our offer.

I believe Dick Russell signaled to you he felt Johnson was right. They want you to stay where you are. We have to have good relationships with those Senators."

When I informed McFarland that Voorhees had withdrawn the offer, McFarland didn't seem to be surprised. I said I hoped that I could remain on his staff. I indicated that I wanted to be helpful to him if he considered me to be useful.

"We can work together, Frank," McFarland said gently. "I'm glad you've made that decision. I need the help of Dick Russell and Lyndon, too. They'll be glad to know you are sticking with me."

McFarland had a genuine humility, an awareness of what he could do and what he couldn't manage. The fact that Russell and Johnson had shown an interest in me obviously had increased my prestige in his eyes. We got along well from then on.

In the confrontation I had with Johnson, I felt that I was confronted by a wild elephant, capable of trampling down anything in its path. The intensity of Johnson's glare was unlike any expression I had seen before on a human face. I thought that Lyndon Johnson would attain any goal he set out to achieve.

When I talked with Bill White later, I found that White had been overpowered by Johnson, too. Although White was an excellent journalist who looked at Senators and the Senate with critical eyes, he had been imbued with Johnson's notion that the Senate was a sacred institution and any one who worked there had a stern duty to fulfill. Although White was a friend of mine and respected my right to make a free decision, he urged me again to remember that I had to assist Ernest McFarland to uphold the highest standards of the Senate. In White's view, my personal happiness had to be subordinated to the needs of the Majority Leader.

White was awed by the energy and dedication Lyndon Johnson poured into the Senate. He indicated to me that Johnson would eventually reach the presidency—and Johnson would then be able to drive through the Congress many of the proposals Truman couldn't get enacted. White told me that Johnson was aware of my abilities. If I played ball with Lyndon, I might be one of his principal aides and advisors when he became the Chief Executive of the United States. I shuddered at that thought.

I realized that Johnson was convinced that a life in politics was a constructive life—a life in which a man could exercise power for the good of the people. I didn't feel a calling to such a life. I had been pulled into the Truman campaign by a friend—and I had never had an ambition to be a professional politician. I was a writer. I wanted to explore every avenue of thought and feeling. I didn't want to spend all my years in helping politicians express the ideas they weren't fully prepared to put into words.

I was afraid Bill White might be right—that Johnson would push his way to the White House. But I believed it would take Johnson some years to get there—and I didn't want to be one of Johnson's men. He might become a much more powerful president than Truman was—and he might also wreck many lives. His thirst for power, his drive to control everything around him, might lead him to a tragic end.

By his insistence on compelling me to stay on the Majority Leader's staff, Johnson altered my life. I felt like a man on a treadmill, going nowhere. I didn't have a hunger for political power, but I did have a desire to engage in significant activities that led to valuable accomplishments. I spent a futile year with Ernest McFarland, striving to get a reluctant Senator to respond to the demands of Truman's staff—in a time when McCarthy was terrifying members of the Senate with a "red scare" and Truman's popularity was falling steeply.

Truman's health insurance plan died in the Congress. So did proposals for middle-income housing and extensive federal aid to education. He tried to form a farm-laborer consumer coalition—and he couldn't overcome the factional squabbles. He was attacked in the press as "a radical liberal" and then denounced by some liberals who felt he didn't have the qualities of Franklin Roosevelt. He went on advocating measures to benefit the whole human family and fought bravely for civil rights. Yet it seemed to me the political process—especially in the Congress—was so badly flawed that I felt ashamed to be involved in it.

In the spring of 1952, I had a brief hope Truman might plunge into another campaign like the one he had mounted in 1948—and bring new vitality into the Democratic Party and the country. But he made it clear he wasn't going to run again. So I decided that I had to end my own painful venture into politics—and to look for other ways of using my talents as a writer.

Then McFarland announced my appointment as the staff director of the Majority Policy Committee, saying that several influential Senators had recommended me for that position. It didn't mean an increase in my salary, but it raised my prestige. I received congratulations from Brien McMahon, Hubert Humphrey, and other Senators I admired. My friends in the White House and the State Department were also pleased. Barbara was delighted by the recognition given to me.

Yet that appointment did not change my inner feeling that I had to move in a new direction. I realized if I accepted the responsibilities of directing the staff of the Policy Committee I might be enmeshed in politics for the rest of my life. I would have to talk about political maneuvers all day long; I would dream about politics, be absorbed in politics, be concerned about one election after another. My friends had already begun to joke with me about my style of speaking—declaring that I was taking on the identity of a Senator.

I had a fascinating but extremely frustrating job. I talked about my frustrations one day with Steve Fitzgerald when he came down from New York to visit me. Fitzgerald had created a Madison Avenue public relations agency and he had many clients. He was an ex-journalist, keenly interested in writing. He said he was expanding his Washington office, and he offered me a place in it. He acknowledged that my contacts on Capitol Hill would be valuable to his agency. He assured me the work would not be arduous—and promised I would have plenty of time to write books. He flattered me by asserting he believed I could have a great future as a writer.

After a dreary session of the policy committee, in which Senators tore various legislative ideas to pieces, I felt angry. I didn't want to spend my remaining years in such meetings. That night I told Barbara I would consider Fitzgerald's offer, because I hoped it would give me the impetus to do my own writing. I was tired of being a "ghost"—preparing statements which carried the names of other men.

My wife was dismayed. She could not understand why I would leave a prestigious position—in which I might have some influence on the Senate—for a precarious spot with a public relations agency. She was doubtful about Fitzgerald's promises. If Fitzgerald lost one or two of his major clients, he might not be able to maintain his Washington office. I might find myself out in the cold.

I recognized the validity of her objections, but I did not heed her advice—although I wished later I had accepted her wise counsel. When I talked with Dr. Schreiber about Fitzgerald's invitation, I emphasized the fact that if I stayed with McFarland I would have to go through a wounding campaign in Arizona—perhaps an ordeal worse than the one I had endured with Lucas in 1950. Schreiber said he thought I was much stronger than I had been then, but he realized I had to decide what seemed best to me.

My sessions with Schreiber always had beneficial effects for me and for my family. He frequently reminded me of how many gifts I had received—especially from the people who loved me. He told me I could learn from my mistakes—and move on to better things. If the Fitzgerald connection wasn't the right one for me, other connections might be made. He saw many avenues available for me.

Yet I had an abysmal hole in me—a fear I was not doing what I had been created to do. I had not written the great books I had intended to write. I was not fulfilling the expectations of the God I had worshiped in my youth, or the expectations of my father and mother, of my teachers, editors, friends, and of myself. I had taken part in a crusade with Harry Truman—and nothing much had come of it.

If I went through the crucible of another campaign—with the atmosphere full of false charges and misleading statements—would I have proved anything? Would the country be any better off? Would the Senate be better? If McFarland defeated Goldwater I would still be on the Senate treadmill, producing ghostly speeches and listening to the windy oratory of other Senators delivering statements written by staff members.

So I made one of the strangest decisions of my life. I told McFarland I had received another offer, and I had decided to end my service on the Senate staff. I was sure he could get someone from Arizona to take my place. I reminded him that it would probably be better for him to have an assistant who could campaign with him in his home state.

McFarland was disturbed by my abrupt declaration. We had become friends, and he had believed I was reasonably happy in my position. He accepted my resignation with reluctance. Bill White and Lyndon Johnson did not attempt to get me to change my mind. White knew I wanted to write books—and he hoped I would have the time to do it.

I think I had a foreboding that McFarland would be beaten by Goldwater and Johnson would become the next Majority Leader. I did not want to be there when that happened. I knew Johnson was rough on his staff members. He was a man willing to browbeat and perhaps even blackmail people to submit to his commands. I did not want to be subjected to his bursts of rage.

I left the spacious office of the Majority Policy Committee and moved into a small suite of rooms rented by the Fitzgerald Company. Fitzgerald's major clients included the National Association of Electric Companies, a lobbying organization representing the private utilities of the United States; the Creole Petroleum Company, a giant subsidiary of the Standard Oil Company of New Jersey; and the Baltimore & Ohio Railroad. The executives of these companies were generally conservative Republications, who thought that "free enterprise" would solve all the nation's problems—and they believed Congress should make it possible for them to thrive and increase their profits year after year.

Although they had opposed Truman in the 1948 election, they expressed admiration for Truman's personal courage and honesty. They were impressed by the fact that I had written speeches for him. They liked the pamphlets and speeches I produced for them. Fitzgerald was pleased by their reactions and indicated I might soon become a partner or a vice president in his agency.

But I realized in a few weeks I had made a mistake. The work I did for Fitzgerald's clients did not give me a sense of satisfaction. In the evenings I wrote chapters of my satirical novel about a Congressional investigation—venting some of the frustrations I had felt on Capitol Hill—and yet the development of the novel did not relieve my depression. I did not see any light on the horizon.

From time to time, sitting in my quiet office, I tried to pray. In Chicago I had asked God to forgive me for my unbelief, and Sister Mary Alcoque had been certain that God would answer that prayer. She was positive that God would listen to me. My wife prayed daily, and she felt the presence of God. I didn't. I tried to meditate, to become aware of a loving Creator—to feel a response, to be calmed and centered in a Divine Being. But I felt nothing.

One rainy day I returned to that office from a luncheon meeting and looked at the messages a secretary had stacked on my desk. I didn't want to respond to any of them. I sat there, paralyzed. Then the door opened and a man in a raincoat came into my office, dripping water. It was Jim Lanigan, the chief assistant to Averell Harriman, the Director of Mutual Security in the Truman administration.

"Come on, Kelly," Lanigan said. "I've come to get you out of here. Harriman's going to run for President and we want you with us. Dave Lloyd and Charlie Murphy think you could help us. Averell talked to Truman and Harry encouraged him to jump in. Adlai Stevenson doesn't seem eager to run, and Truman is backing Harriman."

I couldn't believe he was serious. Lanigan's statement reminded me of the call I had received from the White House in 1948—the call which had brought me to Washington. My life seemed to be disrupted often by my friends. Kenny Birkhead had pulled me into the Truman campaign. Al Vigderman had persuaded Senator Lucas to invite me to join his staff. I couldn't let Lanigan get me into another adventure.

It didn't seem probable that the thin nervous man who faced me— a man named Lanigan, who had a puddle of rain around his shoes— could be an answer to prayer.

"Jim, what are you talking about?" I shook my head. "I just took this job with Fitzgerald. You know that Stevenson will take the Democratic nomination, after a lot of see-sawing. Trying to get it for Harriman is a wild goose chase."

Lanigan grinned. "You like wild geese, Kelly. You're one yourself. If you tell Fitzgerald you'll be working for a candidate backed by Truman, he'll give you a leave of absence. If Harriman did win, Fitzgerald would have a friend in the White House. You would be the press secretary to the President. That's what we have in mind for you."

"You're writing a scenario," I protested. "This isn't Hollywood, Lanigan. What have you been smoking?"

"Just cigarettes," Lanigan said. "Come with me to Harriman's office. You had him up for breakfast once with McFarland. He remembers that. I want you to talk with Averell. We'll have a ball, man. Averell can finance his own campaign. He's got the chips. Talk with Averell, and then we'll call Fitzgerald."

I knew Fitzgerald well enough to be sure he would probably encourage me to join the Harriman drive. His business was built on contacts, and I would get many contacts in a Harriman swing across the country. "All right, we'll talk with Averell," I said. "He'd make a fine President. And Stevenson might decide to wait four more years. Eisenhower will get the Republican nomination and I don't think Adlai believes he can beat Ike. But Harriman might." "That's what I figured," Lanigan said. "Truman figured it that way, too."

I thought I had put the political life behind me. But I had been deeply impressed by the conversation McFarland and I had enjoyed with Harriman at our breakfast meeting. A key figure in Franklin Roosevelt's administration, Harriman had been the chief administrator of the Lend-Lease program in Europe, the U.S. ambassador to the Soviet Union in the crucial years of World War II, the American ambassador to Britain, Secretary of Commerce, a director of the European Recovery project, and head of the Mutual Security Administration. He had become one of Truman's principal advisors. I felt he had the broad range of experience needed by a President to take over the White House when Truman retired.

"Truman's endorsement will help him, but it won't put him over," I said. "Kefauver has already won some delegates, and Barkley wants it, too." "Maybe it will be a tough fight," Lanigan conceded. "But Averell has enough support and enough money to pull it off. Frank Roosevelt, Junior, has agreed to be his campaign chairman. You can be his Washington director. I don't want any title."

I succumbed to the temptation. I pulled my raincoat and hat from a closet, and rode with Lanigan in a taxi through a heavy rain to Harriman's office. Harriman told me he would base his speeches and statements on Roosevelt's New Deal and the Truman program. The fact that one of Roosevelt's sons would be his national chairman certainly would draw attention from Democratic leaders. He had gained the backing of key people in New York, his home state, and New York would have a large number of delegates at the Democratic convention in Chicago.

Harriman said he needed someone who knew many Senators, someone in good standing with Truman's staff, someone who had public relations ideas and excellent contacts with the press. He thought I fitted that description. He said that Lanigan would be his personal advisor but he would expect me to manage his Washington operation. He offered me a starting salary of $20,000 annually—more than I was receiving from the Fitzgerald agency—and said he would ask Fitzgerald to make me available as soon as possible.

"I had resolved to get out of politics," I said. "But I'm honored to be with you. You have the qualifications to be a great President. I hope we can get enough delegates to see that." "It won't be easy," Harriman said. "I've never run for any office. I don't have a record to show that I'm electable."

Lanigan intervened. "The Republicans will probably go for Eisenhower. He has never been elected to anything either."

When I told my wife about the leap I wanted to make, I thought she might chide me. But she admired Harriman; he had an enormous range of experience and he had not been touched by any scandal. Fitzgerald also said he understood why I could not resist Harriman's offer. He assured me I could return to his agency if Harriman did not get the Democratic presidential nomination in July.

After I attended several meetings with Lanigan and Democratic leaders in the District of Columbia, we decided to put Harriman into a primary contest with Estes Kefauver to see how many votes he might gather. While I was helping to organize that effort, I had a phone call from Senator McFarland, who informed me that Senator Russell had decided to enter the race for the presidency. McFarland said that Russell wanted me to be the press officer in his national campaign. "I can't do that," I said. "I've already become the Washington director for Harriman."

McFarland made a derisive sound. "Why the hell did you get into that, Frank? You should have talked to me first. Harriman can't make it. He doesn't have the weight that Dick Russell does. He has never been elected to anything. He can't just jump into the presidency."

"Truman is backing Harriman," I said. "He can't back Russell, even though he likes Dick. You know how much Truman cares about civil rights. Russell won't get votes in the northern and western states. He can't win."

McFarland sighed. "Well, good luck to you, Frank. I'll see you at the convention. Harriman won't get the nomination and maybe Dick Russell won't make it either, but he'll be a real contender." "I appreciate your thinking of me," I said. "I'm deeply grateful for your friendship. I hope you'll beat Goldwater."

A few days later I received a telephone call from another friend, W. McNeil Lowry, the chief Washington correspondent of the Cox newspapers. Lowry said the International Press Institute was going to make a global study of the flow of news, using a large financial gift from the Ford Foundation. He invited me to work with him as one of the directors of that project. The idea of that study intrigued me. But I reminded Lowry I couldn't think about any project until I knew the outcome of the Democratic convention in July.

"This study won't begin until September," Lowry said. "Would you be willing to take it then, if Harriman doesn't get nominated? We'd want you to be in New York, working with Lester Markel, the Sunday editor of the Times, who is keenly interested in the project." "Let me talk about it with Barbara," I said. "She won't be happy about our moving anywhere."

When I described my conversation with Lowry to Barbara, she was immediately interested. Barbara admired Mac Lowry and his vivid wife, Elsa. She didn't want to face another drastic change in our life. In spite of that, she encouraged me to tell Lowry that I would take part in the International Press Institute study if Harriman wasn't the Democratic candidate for president.

Harriman, Lanigan and I flew around the country in a chartered plane, trying to persuade Democratic delegates to support his candidacy. He referred frequently to Truman's liberal proposals, and declared he would try to carry them forward if he became president. As I traveled with him, I was increasingly convinced he had the knowledge, the international recognition, the personal persuasiveness, that might enable the United States to move toward a peaceful co-existence with the Soviet Union—whose leaders respected him. I hoped the delegates in Chicago would sense he had the qualities needed to lead America and the world into a new era of progress.

But, ultimately, the delegates at the Democratic convention turned to Adlai Stevenson, and I was asked to join Stevenson's campaign staff—and I refused. Stevenson was critical of Truman and reluctantly acknowledged that Truman should have a part in the 1952 struggle. I had come to Washington to serve under Truman's banner—and I decided the time had come to return to journalism in New York.

I never went back into politics. As the years passed, I became more and more aware of Truman's greatness and his impact on people around the world. In part two of this book, I have attempted to present Truman's philosophy—and the deep compassion of an extraordinary man, who kept growing in wisdom throughout his life.

PART TWO

A MEDITATION ON HARRY TRUMAN—THE MAN AND HIS ACCOMPLISHMENTS AS A PRESIDENT WHO FORESAW A GREAT FUTURE FOR HUMANITY

CHAPTER THIRTEEN

HIROSHIMA, NAGASAKI, AND HELL—TRUMAN'S BURDEN

IF HELL IS A PLACE OF INESCAPABLE TORMENTS—a state of agony that never ends—war is a state of suffering comparable to hell. Harry Truman went through hell on a battlefield in France in World War I, when German shells were falling all around him. Other men were killed or wounded but he was not physically injured, although the screaming shells burned forever in his memory. From that day onward, he believed God had a special mission for him to perform—a mission that would be gradually revealed in the course of his life.

He had not aimed to become President of the United States, and when the death of Franklin Roosevelt put him in that office he shuddered and prayed. He even asked for the prayers of the newspapermen who watched him struggling with his responsibilities. He prayed himself, often and fervently. In every situation he worked hard, he did his best, he acknowledged his obligations to perform his duties, but he also recognized that his life was shaped by a Creator who was in charge of the whole Universe.

In his diary, he recorded this prayer: "Oh Almighty and everlasting God, creator of Heaven, Earth and the Universe, help me to be, to think, to act what is right because it is right; make me truthful, honest, and honorable in all things...." He did not refer to God as the creator of hell. Judging from what he said to me, I think he believed that men created hell on earth—and possibly a state of eternal torment for themselves.

Through his mother, he had received stern moral teachings. Certain things were right and other things were wrong—and she expected him to know right from wrong. In a way, his mother's voice was the voice of God. When he spoke of her, there was a reverence that indicated how he felt about her—almost a tone of awe. She had placed in his heart a feeling that he had to do what was right and take the consequences, whatever they might be.

When Truman talked with me in the Oval Office in the spring of 1949—in an interview cited eartlier—I told him I wanted to get an understanding of how he had made the major decisions of his presidency, particularly on the use of atomic bombs against Japan and his authorization of an airlift to break the Soviet blockade of Berlin.

"I get the best advice I can and then I try to do what's right," Truman said quickly. "I remember what my mother told me."

"I've heard that all of your advisors urged you to drop the bombs on Japan," I said. His face tightened. I saw the anguish in his eyes. I realized that Harry Truman knew he would always have to live with the results of his decisions—and historians would judge him for generations to come. He had heeded the advice of Secretary of War Stimson and General George Marshall, who had convinced him it was right for him to destroy two Japanese cities, but the burden would always be on his shoulders.

Truman leaned toward me. "Frank, you remember what old General Sherman said about war. War is hell. I knew it. We were burning up thousands and thousands of Japanese men, women and children with our B-29 raids, using fire bombs. I hoped the atomic bombs would get the Japanese emperor to surrender—to end that hell. And he did. But it was terrible to have to kill all those people in Hiroshima and Nagasaki."

I had experienced the fires of war, too. I remembered the men I had seen in flames on a burning oil tanker, when it had been struck by a Nazi torpedo launched by a submarine against that ship. I remembered the wounded men I had seen in England and Normandy—men without arms or legs, men without eyes, men who shrieked with pain and rage. I remembered the nightmares my father had brought home from the first World War—endless dreams of stabbing German soldiers with a bloody bayonet.

"I was in the army when you made the announcement about Hiroshima," I said. "I was glad we had atomic bombs. I realized then the war would be over soon. I wouldn't have to go to the Pacific." Truman

191

nodded. "I didn't want any more of you boys to be killed or wounded," he said.

I forgot I was supposed to be there as a reporter, as a objective interviewer expected to dig deeply into Truman's mind. I was a war veteran talking to another war veteran who happened to be the President of the United States.

The details of that meeting with Truman were burned into my memory. It gave me a sense of companionship with that lonely man, a sense of sharing the weight he had been compelled to carry. Since my childhood, I had felt a responsibility for everything that happened. He carried the world on his shoulders. I had tried to carry it, too. I hoped that I would one day be able to describe—after many years of thinking and meditating—what he had faced in the presidency and the terrible steps he had taken to lift humanity out of the hell created by voracious human beings.

When I talked with him that day I was not aware he had Tennyson's poem in his wallet—the poem predicting the eventual abolition of war and the creation of "the Federation of the World." But his concern about the Japanese who were being consumed by fire bombs—as well as his concern for all the people of the earth, as expressed in his inaugural address—impressed upon me the depth of his feelings and the range of his vision.

Although he had not graduated from any college and he was not regarded as a scholar in any field, he had read more about the history of many nations than most of his predecessors in the White House. The extent of his knowledge was revealed in the course of his conversation. It was apparent he continually tried to expand his comprehension and his compassion.

When Truman spoke of the hellish nature of war, I was well aware of the fact that he read the Bible often—and pondered the meanings of the Scriptures. He was fully familiar with the descriptions of "hell" as a place of perpetual fire and punishment. I was also sure the preachers Truman had heard in his youth had painted vivid pictures of what such torment meant.

Truman had been in Potsdam, Germany, when he had received a dispatch indicating that an atomic bomb had been tested successfully. He had gone there to participate in a conference with Joseph Stalin and Winston Churchill.

"While you were in Potsdam you had a report on the testing of a weapon in New Mexico," I said. "Did you say anything to Marshal Stalin about it?"

"My main purpose in Potsdam was to get Stalin to enter the war against Japan as soon as possible," Truman reminded me. "Our military boys thought we'd need action by the Russians to convince the Japanese that they had to surrender. Those boys weren't sure the atom bombs would be enough to get the Emperor to quit. I just told Stalin we had tested a new type of bomb, probably the most powerful bomb every devised. But I didn't say it released atomic energy. That was secret." "Did Stalin make any comment?" I asked.

"Old Joe had a poker face," Truman said. "I couldn't tell what he thought of the news I gave him. He did say he hoped we would use that bomb against the Japanese right away. He knew there were fanatical officers in Japan who didn't want to give up."

I learned later that Soviet spies had fully informed Stalin about the American atomic project. At the time of the Potsdam meeting, the Soviets were striving to develop atomic weapons with the aid of German scientists they had captured. Truman, of course, did not realize how much Stalin knew when he talked with the Soviet dictator at that conference in 1945.

On July 16, 1945, one day before his initial conversation with Stalin, Truman had ridden in an automobile through the ruins of Berlin He witnessed the total devastation of the center of that huge city—caused by Allied bombers and Soviet artillery. The enormous destructive power of "conventional weapons" was evident in the smashed buildings.

Truman saw a long line of old men, women and children stumbling through the wrecked streets, carrying a few of their possessions. He noted: "In that two-hour drive I saw evidence of a great world tragedy, and I was thankful the United States had been spared the unbelievable devastation of this war...."

In the interview he gave me Truman did not mention his grim tour of Berlin, but it certainly could have been a factor in his willingness to use atomic bombs as instruments to end the hellish situation in the Far East. He knew the air force generals under his command were prepared to set fire to every city, town and village in Japan.

Truman realized that the German civilians he had seen in the ruins of Berlin were victims of the war—and so were the Japanese burned alive by the fire bombs dropped upon their cities by B-29 bombers. The Germans and the Japanese had brought destruction upon themselves by following cruel leaders and supporting or participating in crimes against other people. But Truman saw no sense in a continuation of the policy of hurling fire from the sky upon them. He was not a detached Commander in Chief of the American armed forces. He was an ex-soldier who carried in him vivid memories of the torments of the fiendish slaughter called war.

While Truman spoke with me that day, I remembered he had expressed his feelings about the impact of atomic energy in a speech he had delivered in Milwaukee in 1948. He did not simply refer to the nuclear weapons as instruments which had speeded up the end of the Pacific fighting. He revealed he had become increasingly aware of the endless repercussions from the release of the atomic fire.

"The future of every one of us depends on whether atomic energy is used for good or evil," Truman said somberly. "There are three fundamental facts about atomic energy that each of us should understand. First of all, the atomic bomb is the most terrible and devastating weapon that man has ever contrived. Second, because atomic energy is capable of destroying civilization, it must be controlled by international authority. And third, if properly controlled, atomic energy can enrich human life for all the generations to come...."

In that statement, Truman described his efforts to develop a plan for the international control of such energy. He declared that the United States had offered to stop making atomic bombs when an effective control system had been established. He asserted that the majority of the countries represented on the United Nations Atomic Energy Commission reached an agreement on a control plan—but it was rejected by the Soviet Union.

Truman spoke hopefully about the possibilities of producing power from nuclear plants. He added, "Great progress is being made in the use of atomic materials for research in biology and medicine. Here, we are warring against cancer and the other diseases which take their terrible toll of lives... Atomic materials are also opening up tremendous new possibilities in agricultural and industrial research...."

In my interview with him, I did not question the optimistic statements he had made about the peaceful uses of atomic energy. At that time, I shared his view about the beneficial results that could come from it.

Like Truman, I wanted to believe that his decision to smash Japanese cities with atomic bombs had been made for justifiable reasons. In a talk given in Toledo in October 1948 he spoke vehemently about what he had gone through in making it: "I studied that question with everything I had. I called in the most able men that I could get who would give me advice... And the judgment of all these able and distinguished men was that it would be a life-saving proposition to bring the war to a close as quickly as possible...."

He never indicated he had considered the possibility of asking for the advice of leaders of other nations before he made that decision. He felt that God had enabled the United States of America to develop atomic weapons. He was the Commander in Chief of the American armed forces; therefore, he felt he had the freedom and the responsibility to decide what to do with those awesome weapons.

Truman knew that the Japanese were toppling into defeat. If the messages transmitted by the Allied nations to the Japanese leaders had guaranteed the retention of the Japanese Emperor, Japan might have surrendered in June or July—and the decision to use atomic bombs would not have been forced upon Truman. But the assurance about the Emperor had not been given, and the Japanese continued to fight furiously.

Even after the city of Hiroshima had been virtually obliterated by the first nuclear bomb, there were military leaders in Japan who resisted the idea of surrender. In his fine biography of Truman, David McCullough used documents obtained after the war to describe what occurred in Tokyo in the final days: "General Anami, the war minister, called for one last great battle on Japanese soil—as demanded by the national honor, as demanded by the honor of the living and the dead. 'Would it not be wondrous for this whole nation to be destroyed like a beautiful flower?' he asked. But when the news of Nagasaki was brought in, the meeting was adjourned to convene again with the Emperor that night in the Imperial Library. In the end, less than twenty-four hours after Nagasaki, it was Hirohito who decided. They must, he said, 'bear the unbearable' and surrender...."

In a sense, Harry Truman had to "bear the unbearable" when he made what he called "the most terrible decision that any man in the history of the world had to make." He was the Chief Executive of the American nation. He felt he had acted as the representative of all the people in that huge country. Under the Constitution developed in Philadelphia in 1787, the entire "executive power" of the United States was centered in the person who held the office of President.

On the other side of the world, a small Japanese man named Hirohito—who had the title and authority of Emperor—acted for the Japanese nation by deciding to bring the hellish war to an end. Hirohito risked his throne to make that decision. There were officers who wanted to make him a prisoner—and keep him from speaking to the Japanese people. But their plot failed, and the Japanese obeyed the orders of their Emperor.

The atomic attacks on Hiroshima and Nagasaki occurred in the context of the climactic events of 1945. Americans and their allies were weary of the war—and immensely angry at the Japanese for their fanatical insistence on a continuation of battles which cost thousands of lives. In America and Europe, Truman was hailed for his decisive action.

Later on, the validity of his decision was challenged even by commentators who admired him. In a book entitled *The Pathology of Power*, Norman Cousins wrote: "The decision of President Truman to drop atomic bombs on large aggregations of human beings may be a significant example of the way even good men can incorrectly assess and mishandle unprecedented power... It is possible that nothing that has happened since 1945 calls for more thought by the American people than that decision. It represented more than an effort to bring about a rapid end to the war with Japan. It had implications on almost everything that has happened since...."

I certainly agreed with the statement of Cousins that Truman's action had "implications on almost everything" that occurred in the subsequent years. I have been thinking about Truman's decisions for almost fifty years, and I am sure that Truman himself was not fully aware of the repercussions from what he did. My face-to-face meetings with him—in that conversation in the Oval Office in 1949, and in the reception he gave my family in 1951—convinced me that he was a man who cared about saving Japanese lives as well as the lives of Americans, a man who took tremendous responsibilities for decisions he had to make in tragic situations.

The more I try to judge his actions in 1945—and the more I ponder the words of the Japanese general who was apparently willing to have his whole nation "destroyed like a beautiful flower"—the more I wonder whether any President would have made a different decision than the one he took. In the battle for Okinawa, many Japanese pilots committed suicide by diving their planes directly upon American ships, inflicting severe sufferings on themselves as well as upon the Americans in those vessels. There were high-ranking Japanese officers who talked about "luring" the United States into an invasion of their homeland which might have cost huge numbers of lives—far more than the numbers killed in Hiroshima and Nagasaki. Truman had to consider all of those factors.

I believe that George Elsey, one of Truman's aides with whom I worked in 1948, was right when he described World War II as "a horrible thing." Truman had lived through two global conflicts—and he knew that those savage struggles had killed millions of people and had driven millions of families from their homes. He had volunteered for military service in 1917, responding to the passionate declarations of President Woodrow Wilson, who had called the first World War "a war to end war" and a crusade "to make the world safe for democracy." But he had realized that wars devoured humanity. He felt that the time had come to put an end to international violence.

Truman's use of those bombs against Japan may have been a crucial factor in preventing a third world war. I began to think of that possibility in 1983 when I went to Moscow as a member of a citizens' committee to take part in dialogues with Soviet leaders. The Soviets appeared to be extremely anxious to avoid a nuclear conflagration. The destruction of Hiroshima and Nagasaki had shown them that the United States was capable of using such weapons in a military conflict. They spoke urgently about the necessity of getting rid of such weapons as rapidly as possible.

After those sessions in Moscow, I returned to America with a determination to promote nuclear disarmament. I felt the Soviets were ready to abandon the "cold war" which had led to an arms race for three decades. Soviet citizens told our group that the expensive competition with the United States could not be maintained. Rockets and atomic warheads made both nations far more vulnerable than they had been in any other age. I found Soviet leaders were just as terrified of American power as Americans were of Soviet strength.

Two years after those dialogues in Moscow, Mikhail Gorbachev became the head of the Soviet Union—and his overtures to Britain and the United States set in motion a sequence of events which opened the way for a new era of cooperation. The Soviet Union collapsed and the United States established friendly relations with the governments of Russia, the Ukraine, and other countries which emerged from the wreckage of the Soviet structure. The peril of nuclear annihilation receded, although thousands of atomic weapons remained in existence.

In the interview he gave me in 1949, Truman had predicted many of the amazing developments which occurred in the 1980's. He had declared in his inaugural address in January of that year: "The supreme need of our time is for men to learn to live together in peace and harmony." When he spoke with me, he expressed confidence in the ability of human beings to learn that lesson. The towers of radioactive smoke which arose over Hiroshima and Nagasaki had shown what could happen if humanity engaged in a brutal struggle, using such weapons. Truman had forced the leaders of many nations to see the necessity for abolishing war.

Truman's experience in the battle of the Argonne in France in 1918, when he came close to death, had deep effects upon his life and his thinking. In his first campaign for a public office—in 1922, when he ran for a county judgeship with the support to the Pendergasts—Truman was criticized because he admitted he had voted for a Republican, John Miles, in a previous election. Miles had demonstrated his bravery on the battlefield in France.

"I have seen him in places that would make hell look like a playground," Truman said. "I have seen him stick to his guns when Frenchmen were falling back. I have seen him hold the American line when only John Miles and his three batteries were between the Germans and a successful counterattack. He was of the right stuff and a man who didn't vote for his comrade under circumstances such as these would be untrue to himself and to his country."

Harry Truman was true to the men who served with him under artillery fire. He was true to his friends, true to his beliefs, true to the principles imbued in him by his mother and his teachers. When he came home from France, he felt that God had protected him from a violent death—and he had an obligation to use the extended life he had been given to work for peace and justice.

In the decades of this century, men have been forced to define masculinity in a variety of ways. Truman helped me to see that a real man could be strong and compassionate, ready to stand up for human rights and courteous to every human being, ready to defend his country and yet eager to build a global community. He was a warrior who hated war, a politician who transcended politics, a man who lived simply, a public servant who was actually grateful for all the opportunities he had to serve other people.

When I worked for him in the 1948 electoral struggle, I believed I was doing him a favor. I wasn't prepared for the profound impact Truman had on my conceptions of the meaning of life. But now I know that I am forever linked with him—and I am glad.

CHAPTER FOURTEEN

RISKING WAR BY DOING WHAT HIS MOTHER TAUGHT HIM—HOW TRUMAN BROKE THE BERLIN BLOCKADE

ON THE DAY WHEN TRUMAN SPOKE TO ME about his anguished decision to use atomic bombs against Japan, I asked him about another controversial action he had taken. In 1948 he had ordered a round-the-clock airlift of supplies into Western Berlin after the Soviets had clamped a blockade on the city, refusing to allow American and British freight trains to cross the Soviet-occupied zone in Germany. The British had joined in the operation—and Allied planes had carried millions of tons of food and fuel into the western sector of Berlin, enabling the people there to survive.

"The Soviets were making some threatening statements when you decided to try the airlift," I said. "Wasn't there a risk of war then? Were you prepared for that?"

I remembered how many people had been alarmed by Truman's action. The United States wasn't psychologically ready for an armed conflict with a formidable adversary. The nation had reduced its military services drastically after the surrenders of Nazi Germany and Japan. But the Soviets had continued to maintain large armies in Europe.

"I didn't intend to get into a war," Truman said. "I didn't think the Russians were ready for another struggle. We certainly didn't want one. But we had to do what was right. That was what my mother taught me. You know it's true, too, You have to do what's right."

I thought of the millions of people who might have been killed in a military confrontation with the Soviet Union. Would historians have felt that Truman was justified in taking such a risk? Was the supplying of a German city worth such a dangerous action, when millions of citizens in Allied countries were still mourning the victims of German aggression? I wondered whether Truman's mother would have been willing to accept responsibility for such a perilous decision.

From what I had read about her, I was sure that Truman's mother had not expected him to become president. She gave him the best advice she could for all the circumstances he might encounter in whatever job he held. She insisted he could tell right from wrong—and she wanted him to be on the right side of everything.

Truman told me about his discussions with the Joint Chiefs of Staff—or "the military boys," as he called them. He said he asked General Lucius Clay, who had been dealing with the Russians in Germany, whether there were indications the Soviets were mobilizing for a full-scale showdown. Clay was reassuring; he reported that the Soviets were just trying to assert control over the entire city of Berlin. The Soviet armies had taken Berlin without participation from American or British troops. The whole city was in a zone occupied by Soviet forces.

"I didn't think that the Russian capture of Berlin gave them a right to blockade it," Truman said. "We had done our share to smash the Nazis; the Russians had been linked with us in the Allied command in Berlin. They couldn't convince me they had a right to squeeze us out. We had a right to be there. I asked the military boys to supply the city with planes."

I asked him what reactions he had received from the participants in that session in Oval Office. He said that General Hoyt Vandenberg, the Air Force chief of Staff, was concerned about concentrating so many planes in one area of the world. If the Soviets brought about a crisis at another flash point in Europe or Asia, there wouldn't be enough planes immediately available to counter them. "I told Vandenberg to let me worry about that," Truman said.

Under the Constitution, of course, Truman was the Commander in Chief. Generals and admirals might raise questions, but he expected and got their obedience when he had reached a decision.

When Truman initiated the Berlin airlift on July 22, 1948, he was engaged in a bruising struggle to retain his place in the White House.

Judging by the polls of George Gallup and Elmo Roper, he did not have the support of a majority of prospective voters at that time. In spite of his weak political position, he expected that his authority as the incumbent Chief Executive would be respected—and it was.

When he wrote about his Berlin decision in his memoirs—published six years after my 1949 interview with him—Truman did not refer to the influence of his mother. He did record the fact that General Vandenberg had misgivings about the airlift. He noted: "... Vandenberg interjected that it would not be possible unless additional airfield facilities were constructed in Berlin. General Clay pointed out that he had already selected a site for an additional field and that construction, using German manpower, could begin at once. General Vandenberg then assured me that the Air Force would devote its entire energy to the carrying out of my order."

Truman's action saved the people of western Berlin from starvation and collapse. His decision also affected the lives of millions of people in many countries. If a war had occurred, the people of the world would have suffered grievously. Truman was concerned about the whole human family, but he did not contemplate an international referendum on what course should have been taken to break the Soviet blockade. He made the Berlin decision with deep confidence in his own judgment of how the Soviets would respond to it.

Perhaps his confidence was based on his belief that the United States in 1948 had the only atomic weapons in existence. The Soviets still had mighty armies in Europe, but those armies could have been wiped out by nuclear bombs. Truman did not mention the atomic weapons as a factor in his decision, but the existence of those weapons may have convinced the Soviets that they could not allow a military conflict with the United States to occur. Through their spies, the Soviets undoubtedly knew Truman was trying to rescue western Berlin without a war.

On that day when he described to me how he had overcome the doubts of General Vandenberg about the airlift, I saw the steely strength in his face. He clearly believed he had been empowered by his fellow citizens to make final decisions. I learned through the years that Truman acted in the tradition of George Washington, who had set the patterns of behavior for strong presidents. Washington interpreted the Constitution to mean that the presidency was an independent branch of government—with direct authority from the people to act separately from the Congress and the Supreme Court.

In addition to listening to the wisdom of his mother, Harry Truman had studied the records of all the men who had preceded him in the White House. He particularly admired Andrew Jackson, a rough-and-ready leader, who ignored a resolution of the House of Representatives and seized federal funds from the Bank of the United States—and also acted to prevent South Carolina from seceding from the federal union. Dismissing his critics in those cases, Jackson had declared: "It was settled by the Constitution, the laws, and the whole practice of the government that the entire executive power is vested in the President...."

Truman also accepted the idea of James K. Polk, who said: "The President represents in the executive department the whole people of the United States, as each member of the legislative department represents portions of them...." He knew that Abraham Lincoln held that there were no legal limits on a Chief Executive when a president was preserving, protecting and defending the Constitution. He had watched Franklin D. Roosevelt expand the functions of the presidency in peace and war.

The Berlin airlift was hailed by many people in Europe as a strong sign of American determination to prevent Soviet domination of that continent. Month after month, Allied planes roared over the heads of Soviet soldiers who encircled Berlin. The Soviets did not open fire on any of those planes. It soon became evident that the Soviets did not want to have a showdown with the United States.

Truman noted later: "The Kremlin began to see that its effort to force us out was doomed. Russia's toughness and truculence in the Berlin matter led many Europeans to realize the need for closer military assistance ties among the western nations, and this led to discussion which eventually resulted in the establishment of the North Atlantic Treaty Organization (NATO). Berlin had been a lesson to all."

In 1949, when the Soviets abandoned the blockade, Truman expressed his admiration for the airlift: "Technically, it was an extremely tough job—so difficult that even the Air Force chiefs themselves at first had serious doubts that it could be done. It proved a beacon light of hope for the peoples of Europe." His decision to do what was right—simply because it was right, as his mother put it—had brought immense benefits.

While he was campaigning in 1948, Truman received frequent reports on the Berlin situation. He rejected suggestions that he should break off negotiations because of the surly behavior of the Russians. He said in his memoirs: "These people did not understand that our choice was only between negotiations and war. There was no third way. As long as the Russians were willing to continue talks—however futile—there would be no shooting."

Those of us who worked on Truman's speeches in that campaign had no hints from him that a war might occur. He did not cite his decision to supply Berlin by air as a means of getting votes. He did realize, however, that the American people wanted peace—and he reiterated that the "heart and soul" of his international policies came from his resolution to maintain peace.

In New York City on October 29, a few days before the election of 1948, he spoke somberly, "The President is the servant of the American people. He must leave no stone unturned in expressing their will for peace.... I will always explore every possible means, no matter how difficult or how unconventional, for reaching agreement.... I welcome the abuse that is showered upon me by those who have made up their minds that war is inevitable. I do not believe that war is inevitable...."

Although Truman's policies were viewed in Europe as strong and effective, he was denounced in the 1948 electoral struggle as a man who tried to appease the Soviets. Some Republican leaders declared it was useless to try to reach agreements with the Soviets, because the agreements would not be kept.

In his New York speech, Truman asked: "Do they fully understand that the stakes in this matter are war or peace, life or death, not only for ourselves and our children, but for our civilization? Do they regard it as nothing more than a campaign issue?"

Although he stayed steadily on a bold course, the terrible possibility of another war weighed heavily on Truman's mind, day and night. He believed that God had placed the responsibility for humanity's future largely upon him.

"After the first World War, the United States had its first great opportunity to lead the world to peace," Truman declared in that New York address. "I have always believed that it was the will of God at that time that we should enter into and lead the League of Nations. How much misery and suffering the world would have been spared if we had followed Woodrow Wilson!... God willing, we will never make that mistake again."

Truman had successfully opposed the Soviets in Iran, in Greece and Turkey, and in Berlin, and he had gained the support of leaders in other countries because he knew that international cooperation was absolutely essential in preventing armed conflicts. He had placed the Berlin crisis on the agenda of the United Nations. He was determined to make the UN far more effective than the League of Nations had ever been.

In another speech in his 1948 campaign—given in Berkeley, California—Truman placed the problems of the nations in a wide context. He said that "the great issues of world peace and world recovery" should not be portrayed as "disputes solely between the United States and Soviet Union."

"The great questions at stake today affect not only the United States and the Soviet Union," Truman told an attentive crowd in Berkeley. "They affect all nations. Whether it be atomic energy, aggression against small nations, the German or the Austrian peace settlements, or any of the other questions, the majority of the nations concerned have found a common basis for action. But in every case the majority agreement has been rejected, denounced and openly attacked by the Soviet Union and the satellites whose policies it controls...."

Truman insisted that the United States acted for the best interests of people everywhere. When he asserted that "the majority of the nations" favored certain steps, he was confident they were on the constructive side—the American side—and the Soviets with their "satellites" were simply blocking progress. He regarded the Soviet leaders as "pigheaded" or as plotters who sought to bring everybody under communist rule.

From a Soviet perspective, of course, the Truman administration was labeled "aggressive" and accused of attempting to subordinate all nations to the capitalist system. The Soviets regarded the Marshall Plan, which brought economic recovery to Western Europe, as essentially a scheme to tie the European countries to the marketing plans of capitalists. The Soviets were not willing to "negotiate" issues that they regarded as threatening their survival.

Fortunately for Truman, his audacious acts in Europe and Berlin were not directly challenged by Tom Dewey, the Republican presidential candidate in 1948. In capturing the Republican nomination, Dewey had defeated Senator Robert Taft and other isolationists in his own party. He endorsed the Berlin airlift, the Marshall Plan, and the extension of military aid to Greece and Turkey to frustrate the communists there. Dewey also supported the swift recognition of Israel as an independent state in Palestine.

In the 1948 campaign, we seldom referred to Dewey and we did not think about him very often. As the President's men, we poured our energies into stinging lines aimed at the "reactionary Republicans" in the 80th Congress—Senator Taft and his lieutenants. Taft was alarmed by many of Truman's international initiatives. Taft contended that the United States had taken on too many obligations to protect other nations—and should not try to create a new world order. Those of us who labored day and night for Truman were sure we were generally right and the Taftites were generally wrong. In the hectic months during which we fired rhetorical shots at the conservative Republicans, we were inspired by a righteous anger. As liberals, we were determined to beat off the assaults of men who were trying to wreck the structures for a better life created by Franklin Roosevelt and Truman.

I regretted the necessity for the Berlin airlift and Truman's other clashes with the Soviets, and I was disturbed by the rising tension between the United States and the Soviet Union but I hoped Truman's actions would lead to a constructive outcome. In my book entitled *An Edge of Light*, I had described how Truman had managed to get the Soviets to withdraw their troops from northern Iran after a confrontation in 1946. I believed he could get them to back down in Berlin. And he did.

On June 25, 1950, nine months after the Soviets had conceded the futility of the Berlin blockade, communist troops from North Korea poured into the southern section of that country. That invasion violated the agreement Truman and Stalin had reached in the Potsdam conference, designating the 38th Parallel as the dividing line between North and South Korea. The Security Council of the United Nations ordered resistance to the attack, and Truman sent American soldiers into battle under the UN banner.

Although he knew the horrors of war—and he had used atomic bombs against Japan to bring an end to the carnage of World War II—Truman felt he had to move swiftly in Korea to prevent a catastrophic series of events. He thought he had to bear the consequences of risking the lives of many soldiers in order to save humanity from greater evils.

"I felt certain that if South Korea was allowed to fall, communist leaders would be emboldened to override nations closer to our own shores," Truman wrote in his memoirs. "If this was allowed to go unchallenged it would mean a third world war, just as similar incidents had brought on the second world war... It was also clear to me that the foundations and principles of the United Nations were at stake...."

Truman apparently believed the Soviet leaders in Moscow had approved the action of the North Koreans. He assumed that the attack on South Korea was part of a global plan to expand communism. Commentators in recent years, with access to documents available after the breakup of the Soviet Union, have indicated that the invasion was actually undertaken by Korean leaders without the full backing of Stalin. While Stalin wanted to extend communism to many countries, he was extremely cautious about sanctioning military actions.

Deeply influenced by his reading of history, Truman saw a parallel between the communists led by Stalin and the Nazis led by Adolf Hitler.

Acting on that view, he came to believe that his decision to aid South Korea was the most important one he made during his years in the presidency. By ordering American forces to serve under the auspices of the United Nations, he believed he had prevented the possible decline and dissolution of the UN.

Truman did not ask Congress for a declaration of war against North Korea, but his strong response to the onslaught of the North Koreans received widespread approval initially from Republicans as well as Democrats. In the 1950 political campaign—as I discussed earlier—the Korean war became a bitter source of discord and debate, resulting in the defeats of some Democratic senators.

Although his Korean decision eventually caused a steep drop in his popularity—and was a factor in the election of a Republican president in 1952—Truman never abandoned his conviction that he had done the right thing in resisting the North Korean aggressors. Whether he referred to his mother or not, I am sure that the ethical principles she had instilled in him affected his policy in Korea as much as those principles had shaped his action to help the people of Berlin.

In his farewell address to the American people in January of 1953, a few days before he left the White House, Truman showed his assurance that his commitment of American military forces in Korea had sent a deterrent warning to the Soviets—and had possibly prevented a third world war. The policy had cost the lives of more than 33,000 Americans and casualties totaling more than 135,000, but a global struggle would have cost millions of lives and might have devastated the whole earth. He placed the blame for the Korean tragedy on the shoulders of Soviet leaders.

While Truman was confident that his major decisions would be viewed as largely justified by future historians, he knew he had made his share of mistakes. His loyalty program had damaged many thousands of lives. His creation of the Central Intelligence Agency had led to covert interventions in the affairs of other nations. He revealed his awareness of his blunders in letters to friends, in public statements, and in the interview he gave me in 1949. He did not think he was the best of all possible Chief Executives.

"When Franklin Roosevelt died, I felt there must be a million men better qualified than I to take up the presidential task," Truman declared in his farewell speech. "But the work was mine to do, and I had to do it. And I have tried to give it everything that was in me...."

As I think of him—laboring in loneliness through hard days and nights, giving his duties everything he had to give, compelled to take tremendous risks—I am keenly aware of what an extraordinary man he was, never yielding to despair, never taking an easy way out of the dilemmas he had to confront. He reflected his heritage, the atmosphere of his age, the culture of his time. Yet his thoughts and acts created repercussions which have spread through the generations—and continue to have effects in the United States and other countries.

Many men cast aside the teachings of their youth and show no gratitude for the gifts they received from their parents. Harry Truman always acknowledged the sources of his wisdom.

CHAPTER FIFTEEN

THINKING OF FUTURE GENERATIONS—TRUMAN'S PROPOSAL FOR FINDING THE BEST PRESIDENTIAL CANDIDATES

AS HARRY TRUMAN became increasingly aware of the repercussions of the decision made in the Oval Office of the President, he became humbly conscious of how difficult it was for any man to carry out all the duties involved in that position. He labored at those duties day and night, and he thought about them in the light of all the volumes he had read about previous presidents, ranging from George Washington to Franklin Roosevelt. He became critical of the nominating system which was controlled by the two major political parties.

When he talked with me in 1949, he made it clear that only a few people were usually considered for the presidency and the vice presidency. Shaking his head, he said: "A few governors and senators are often the only ones regarded as potential presidents. The whole process is haphazard, undignified, and subject to corruption. The persons who might be the best leaders for future generations rarely get any attention."

"Committees of citizens should be formed to hunt for the best candidates," Truman told me. "There should be a national discussion of what kind of president we need. We've gone from one crisis to another, and there are going to be tough times ahead. We'll need the finest persons we can find."

I thought that his suggestion was a good one, but I wondered how it could be carried out. The traditions of American politics called for potential presidents to get experience as senators or governors—and then to attract wealthy supporters who could finance national campaigns. A systematic search for possible presidents—conducted by citizens on a nonpartisan basis—might bring some wonderful persons into the limelight but it would be extremely difficult to get them nominated at national conventions.

The presidential contests after Truman left the White House in 1952—in which the power of money and pressure groups became evident—finally impelled me to try to gain the support of citizens for a nonpartisan hunt for candidates of the highest caliber. I wrote a pamphlet about it—a booklet published by the Nuclear Age Peace Foundation.

I pointed out that the need for a Council of Citizens seemed to be greater than ever in the 1990s, when there was a steep decline in the percentage of voters participating in elections. A widespread disillusionment was noticeable, particularly among young people. Ross Perot and others who offered themselves as independent candidates did not arouse the enthusiasm of many voters.

In the conversation with me, President Truman had not attempted to outline the steps that might have to be taken to enable citizens to carry out his idea. In my presentation, I suggested that the Council could focus attention on two basic questions: "What persons should be encouraged to become available as potential presidents? How should presidential campaigns be conducted in order to give the American people—and the people of the world—opportunities to know about the wisest candidates and to foster a series of public discussions with them?"

In my view, public hearings should be held by the Council in all the regions of the United States. Prospective candidates, chosen by the Council on the basis of suggestions drawn from people of all backgrounds, would be asked to speak at these hearings. They would be expected to discuss questions submitted to them in advance by the Council, and then respond to other questions expressed by members of the public gatherings. All of the proceedings would be broadcast—and videotaped for possible sale at minimum cost to all interested persons. Making the tapes available at low prices would enable all citizens to review what the candidates had discussed and to submit questions for additional meetings.

Each candidate would also be interviewed individually for several hours by noted journalists, using biographical information obtained by the Council's research division. The personal interviews would also be videotaped for consideration by the Council and advisors. Excerpts

211

would be broadcast, and would be made available to citizens at low costs.

After a year of such public hearings and individual examinations, the Council would ask the people who had attended the hearings and/or watched the broadcasts or videotapes to respond to surveys, indicating preferences among the candidates. The Council would then present the leading candidates on a series of television and radio programs, with the candidates participating in dialogues with one another. Viewers and listeners would be encouraged to introduce questions through telephone calls.

At the end of this process, the Council would conduct extensive surveys to obtain the rankings of the candidates and their handling of the basic issues regarded as vital by the public. These surveys would not be ordinary opinion polls. They would be designed to compare the ideas and wisdom of the possible candidates with the deepest concerns of the people.

The Council would then call for a Citizens' Assembly, to be held in February or March of the presidential election year. The 5,000 delegates for that Assembly would be chosen by votes at public gatherings in all regions of the United States. The Council would also invite observers from all parts of the world. These observers would have the right to speak on global issues but would not be able to cast ballots in the Assembly procedures.

The eight candidates regarded as the best qualified men and women would be invited to make brief statements to the Assembly. After six days of intensive discussions of the merits of these persons and their views on the major problems confronting the United States and the world, the delegates would vote. The voting would be done openly and individually (not by states or regions) on television. The delegates would vote first for presidential nominees and then for well-qualified candidates for the vice presidency. The results would be tabulated and announced.

During the balloting in the Assembly, members of the radio and television audiences would be asked to indicate their preferences by using toll-free telephone lines provided by the Council. Their votes would also be tabulated and announced on radio and television after the delegates at the Assembly had completed their voting.

The candidates emerging from this process would be placed in nomination at the conventions of the Democratic, Republican, and Independent parties—as possible alternatives to the partisan candidates who had gathered votes from the traditional primaries. The Council would ask delegates at those conventions to put the names of the Assembly-approved candidates under consideration, so that the party conventions would be aware of the high qualifications of those candidates.

After the party conventions had chosen their nominees, the Assembly would be reconvened to review the records of the persons selected. The Assembly would be asked to vote on a possible endorsement of one set of candidates for president and vice president, or to declare that two sets of candidates were acceptable, or to form a campaign committee to launch an intensive effort to elect other candidates who had been ignored or rejected by the political parties.

During the presidential campaign the Council of Citizens and the Assembly could sponsor televised discussions by the potential presidents who had received the largest number of votes in the Assembly and in the results from the responses of people who voiced their views by telephone or e-mail. These "potential presidents" could candidly examine the fundamental issues facing the nation and the world—issues that might be sidestepped or played down by the conventional candidates nominated at the party conventions.

I do not know whether the process I have outlined in this chapter would have the approval of Harry Truman. But his statements to me in the Oval Office stirred a determination within me to discover ways of opening up presidential campaigns to a broad range of candidates who could be the servant-leaders needed in an age of tremendous challenges.

In many ways, Truman was far ahead of the other political leaders of his time. He repeatedly asserted that the President of the United States had to be more than the chief executive of one nation, because the whole world was affected by the actions of that nation. He declared that the president had to heed the needs of all people and work with people all over the earth for the benefit of humanity—to build a global community with justice, peace and security for all.

In 1996 I wrote a series of articles on the Presidency. In the last article, I dealt with the impact of Truman on several generations of

Americans. I reported that people had asked me, "Where are we going to find another Harry Truman?" I responded, "I think Truman would ask: Where are the people who can give new life to our democracy?" In his 1948 campaign, Truman spoke to millions of people—but he also listened to them. He wanted every person to speak freely—and he wanted every voice to be heard.

Truman was inspired by the idea of Servanthood, of a leader chosen to put the needs of the people above his own pride, a leader willing to sacrifice himself to do what has to be done for the good of all, a leader who thinks of succeeding generations, and looks far into the future. He knew that the future of the presidency and the health of humanity depended upon close connections between the people and those called to be their Public Servants.

If Truman could have returned to the world of the 1990s, I think he would have found signs that his faith in the creative capacities of human beings was justified by some achievements. He would be pleased by the steps toward peace in the Middle East, the friendly relations between the United States and the new Russia, the survival of the United Nations, the peaceful end of apartheid in South Africa, the emergence of democratic governments in some areas of South America, Asia and Africa. He would note the efforts to overcome the evils of racism in his own country and elsewhere.

He would have saluted the constructive policies of some of his successors in the Oval Office—the attempts made by Dwight Eisenhower to carry forward the international policies he had initiated; the Peace Corps created by John Kennedy; the "great society programs" of Lyndon Johnson; the educational programs of Bill Clinton; and certainly the Camp David agreement obtained by Jimmy Carter between Israel and Egypt in 1978. The pacts signed by Arab and Jewish leaders in the 1990s would not have surprised him. In 1949 he had told me that Israel and her neighbors would eventually realize that they had to cooperate with one another.

I believe he would have urged all "potential presidents" to continue the extension of scientific and technical assistance to the poor countries. "There are many millions of people who can get out of poverty if we help them with our knowledge," Truman had said. "Aiding them to learn to develop their own resources will do more for them than just giving them cash."

Truman had not seemed to be troubled by any foreboding that the earth's resources might be rapidly exhausted if all nations moved to high levels of economic growth with American aid. He apparently was confident the planet could provide a prosperous life for all people if the essential resources were preserved from generation to generation. He was vehement in proclaiming that those resources had to be protected from corporate "raiders."

His impassioned advocacy of conservation flared brightly in a speech he gave in 1948 at the dedication of a national park in the Everglades section of Florida. He regarded the great parks of America as essential elements in the nation's survival.

"The battle for conservation cannot be limited to the winning of new conquests," Truman declared in that fiery speech. "Public lands and parks, our forests, and our mineral reserves are subject to many destructive influences. We have to remain constantly vigilant to prevent raids by those who would selfishly exploit our common heritage for private gain. Such raids are not examples of enterprise and initiative; they are attempts to take from all the people for the benefit of a few.'

Truman accepted the Biblical story that the Creator had placed the earth in the stewardship of the human race. He was sure the Creator would demand a reckoning from people who damaged the beautiful and productive planet on which they lived.

"The wise use of our natural resources is the foundation of our effectiveness," Truman said in the Everglades park. "The problems of peace, like those of war, require courage and sustained effort. If we wish this nation to remain prosperous, if we wish it still to be the home of the free, we can have it so. But if we fail to heed the lesson of other nations which have permitted their natural resources to be wasted and destroyed, then we shall reap a sorry harvest."

Truman did not live to see the devastation inflicted on the environment by the activities of the industrial and chemical corporations. But it was evident in what he told me in 1949 that he expected future presidents to exert strong leadership in protecting natural resources for the succeeding generations.

Like Jefferson and Lincoln, Woodrow Wilson and Franklin Roosevelt, Harry Truman did not regard politics as a dirty business. He saw it as a noble vocation. He shared the philosophy of Wilson, who once said: "A nation is not made of anything physical." He realized that a nation was made of dreams and desires, of spiritual longings as well as material wants, of the relationships between people who occupied places of power and the people who put them there.

He certainly hoped the presidents who followed him would be aware of the spiritual side of politics. He acknowledged that divine guidance had a significant influence on his own approaches to political and social problems. He prayed that Almighty God would enable him to submerge his personal ambitions and to do what was right because it was right—not for any other reasons.

As I have thought about what Truman said to me—and about the policies he tried to carry out—I have tried to relate his words and actions to the context that existed during the years of his presidency and the changing contexts of subsequent decades. I have tried to present the man and his ideas in the flow of the turbulent times in which he lived—and in the light of subsequent events in a century of wars and revolutions, with changes occurring so rapidly no leader could cope with them.

I have seen Truman in different lights at different stages of my own experiences in various fields in these decades. I continue to be astonished by the range of topics he covered in the interview he gave me in the Oval Office almost fifty years ago. His mind ranged backward and forward—from the depths of history to the visions of a wonderful age expressed in a poem by Alfred Tennyson.

Truman had a sense of belonging to the universe—not simply as a man or as an American, not simply as a president who took humanity into the nuclear age, but as a person with a clear identity, a person with dimensions extending beyond his years on earth, on a voyage of endless discoveries.

CHAPTER SIXTEEN

*TRUMAN TAKES A CHIDING FROM MY MOTHER, AND BLUSHES
WHEN MY SON FACES HIM WITH INDIGNATION*

WHEN TRUMAN TALKED WITH ME about the qualities he considered necessary for future presidents, he didn't mentioned the capacity to be embarrassed by a small boy or the willingness to be chided by the mother of a friend. But he revealed those qualities when he gave my family a warm welcome in the White House on June 26, 1951. He listened intently to my mother's advice, beamed at my wife and my sister, and presented a fountain pen to my five-year-old son with a mischievous grin, suggesting that the pen could be used "to mark up furniture." He blushed and apologized when my son indignantly rejected that idea.

That visit came about because my mother actually believed I was largely responsible for Truman's amazing victory in 1948. She had come to Washington that June with the expectation of having a nice chat with the President—feeling quite sure he would do anything I asked him to do, since I had done so much for him.

"I bought a new dress before I left Kansas City," she announced when she arrived. "I told everybody in my bridge club I would see the President while I was in Washington."

Truman was then dealing with the repercussions of his decision to remove Douglas MacArthur from command of the military forces in the Far East. The Senate was flooded with mail from citizens who wanted Truman to be booted from the White House.

"Mother, he has a lot of things to confront right now," I reminded her. "I don't know whether I can get you an appointment."

My wife intervened with a swift smile. "Dave Lloyd and Charlie Murphy call you three or four times a week about the President's program. Just tell them your mother wants to have a little visit. He likes mothers."

My wife had been impressed by my story about Truman's frequent references to his mother's wisdom. Since Barbara had encouraged me to act with confidence, I telephoned Charlie Murphy and explained to him that my mother was eager to see the President.

"I know how busy he is," I said. "But would it be possible for me to bring her in for a few minutes? She promised her bridge club she would have a little visit with him." Murphy chuckled. "Let me check with the boss."

Three hours later, Murphy called me. "The President says he'll be glad to have a visit with your mother at 4 o'clock on Tuesday afternoon, if that's a good time for her. Let us know."

When I brought the news home that night, my mother nodded happily. Then she looked over at my sister, Kitty, who had traveled to Washington with her. "I'm sure that Kitty will want to be there, too," she said. "Did you ask about that?"

The next day, I spoke to Murphy again. He called back in an hour: "The President says he'll be happy to see your sister, too."

When I came home with that information, Kitty and my mother were delighted. But Barbara seemed to be a bit miffed. "I think I should go, too," Barbara said. "I didn't get a chance to talk to the President during the campaign because I was in New York, looking after Terry." "Certainly you should be with us," my mother said. "And Terry, too."

Once more, I called Murphy. He responded: "So the whole family wants to come. I think the boss will enjoy that." Two hours later, Murphy was on the line. "The President asked me to tell you that you can round up all the Kellys you want to, and he'll meet all of you at Constitution Hall."

"What?" I gasped. Murphy chuckled. "He also said you can bring your whole family to see him on Tuesday." "That's great!" I said. "We'll be there, Charlie."

When I came home and announced that the President would receive all of us, my mother suddenly became very pale. "Oh, how nice," she said. "But I've been thinking about it and I'm getting cold feet. Frank, he's so busy..." I took her hand. "You can't get cold feet now. I've made three phone calls to the White House. He's put it on his calendar."

I wasn't positive that the President had placed us on his appoint-ment list. In fact, I thought we would be slipped in between some of his official visitors. But I didn't want her to back out. She sighed, "Then we'll have to go."

"Don't sound so grim about it," I said. "We'll have a fine time. He knows we're all friends. He likes to visit with friends." "I did want to tell him that our postmen need a raise," my mother said. "I promised my mail man that I'd speak to him about that."

When we arrived at the White House on Tuesday afternoon, Murphy met us and escorted us to the Oval Office. My mother was wearing a fine pair of white gloves. She asked Murphy, "Should I take off a glove before I shake hands with the President?" Murphy seemed to be startled. He replied in a whisper, "I don't know, Mrs. Kelly. I never wear gloves around here myself."

President Truman came around his desk and approached us with a springy stride, his genial face radiating hospitality. He didn't appear to be at all worried about the crises in the world or the sniping at him in the press or the snarling tigers in the Senate who were trying to wound him.

My mother removed a glove and he clasped her hand. As he did so, she said sweetly: "I'm awfully glad that Frank and you won that election." I was utterly astounded and I think I groaned. "Mother, for God's sake!"

The President smiled. The man who had traveled almost 32,000 miles and delivered more than 350 speeches to win an electoral victory did not seem surprised that my mother attributed his triumph to me.

"It was a hard fight but we did win it, Mrs. Kelly," Truman said gen-tly. He turned to me and winked. "Frank, your mother knows we were in it together. Mothers can say anything in this office. My mother didn't hesitate to speak her mind on any occasion."

"It's so nice of you to receive us, President," my mother said. "I know your time is valuable. You're doing very well, too. Of course, you've made a few mistakes..."

"Mother!" I choked, wishing I hadn't arranged her visit to the White House. But Truman gazed at her calmly. "I'm sure I have," he said, nod-ding. "Tell me about some of them, Mrs. Kelly."

"For one thing, you haven't signed a bill passed by Congress to give the postal workers a raise," my mother said. "My postman asked me to speak to you about it. They really need it. I noticed he had a frayed sleeve on his uniform."

"I've got it on my desk right now," the President said. He regarded her with a warm twinkle in his eyes. "You're a good lobbyist, Mrs. Kelly. I'm going to sign that bill."

"Oh, thank you!" my mother exclaimed. She was a compassionate woman, concerned about human needs. During the Depression of the 1930s, she had fed homeless persons who came to the door of her house. She was glad to help her postman.

"Any other things on your mind?" Truman asked her. My mother looked a bit flustered. "I guess I can't think of anything else, just at this time. I don't want to pester you with a lot of problems. I'm sure you are doing the best you can." She looked around. "This is such a beautiful office. I want to remember everything in it. Not many people get to come in here and see where the President works. I know you are very busy, but I knew that Frank could get us in."

"I'm not too busy to see friends," Truman said. "After all, Frank and I won that election—didn't we Frank?" "Yes, sir, we did," I said, responding to Truman's smile. I could see then that he was enjoying himself, and I relaxed.

The President told Barbara and Kitty he was glad they had been able to come, and he inquired about Terry's age. Terry was wide-eyed and silent, staring around the Oval Office. He gazed at the President with a deep silence.

"I want to thank you for all you've done for all of us," Barbara said. "Frank was so fortunate to get a chance to work for you."

Matt Connelly, the President's appointments secretary, suddenly entered the room and announced, "There are a couple of Senators waiting out there, sir."

"Let them wait," Truman said, waving his hand. "I'm talking with some friends here from Kansas City." "Yes, sir," Connelly said, and he immediately retreated.

220

A few minutes later, our visit came to an end. As we moved toward the door, my mother held out a book to the President—a volume entitled *The Truman Program*, containing some of his speeches and messages to Congress.

"Please sit down there at your desk and write an inscription in this book for me," my mother said, thrusting the book into Truman's hands. "The people in my bridge club will never believe I was in your office and talked with you—unless you sign this book and I can show it to them."

Truman laughed. "I know how they are in those bridge clubs," he said. "I guess you'll need some evidence that you were really here."

He returned to his desk, sat down and wrote rapidly in the front of the book. As he did, I thought of how deferential he was to an insistent mother. He was the Commander in Chief of the American armed forces—but he did what she asked him to do.

I knew that men were in combat in Korea at that hour, acting under orders Truman had given. He had plunged American troops into battle there, to do what he regarded as right—to act in accordance with the moral principles he had received from his mother. Thousands of miles from the White House, men were fighting and dying while he wrote an inscription in that book.

My mother's face glowed when she read what he had written: "To Mrs. Kelly with best wishes on her visit with her family to the White House. Harry S. Truman. White House, June 26, 1951." He did not write that she had visited her President. He simply certified that she had visited the Executive Residence and her presence there had been duly acknowledged by the current occupant—a man from Missouri named Truman.

As we moved to leave the Oval Office, Truman took a fountain pen from his desk—a pen bearing the slogan "A Tried Truman for President," which he had used in his 1948 campaign. He handed it to Terry, and beamed down at my silent son. "Now, Terry, that will remind you some day of the time when you were in the president's office," Truman said. He flashed a smile—as one boy to another. "You can use that to mark up the furniture when you get home."

Terry looked up at him with startled indignation. "Eeek!" he responded in a high-pitched voice, turning toward Barbara. "I don't mark up furniture!"

Then a red tide rushed across the face of the President of the United States, and we saw he was blushing. He swung toward Barbara and apologized. "I shouldn't have said that to your little boy," he admitted in a penitent tone. "I'm very sorry. I shouldn't have told him he could do that."

"You were giving him a gift and you wanted him to have fun with it," Barbara said, smiling. "Thank you very much for your kindness. Thank you for the joy you've given to all of us in this visit with you." Truman walked to the door of the Oval Office with us. As he opened the door, he said, "I've enjoyed it, too."

As we left the White House, I noticed Terry was clutching the pen Truman had given to him. We got into our car and drove toward our apartment in Virginia. As we crossed a bridge over the Potomac River, Terry spoke to me in a low voice, as if he was awakening from a strange dream. "Daddy, was that the President of the United States?" he asked me. "It was, son," I answered.

Terry expelled his breath and repeated the words slowly and softly to himself, "The President of the United States...."

When we got home, my mother stretched out on the couch in our living room. Barbara and Kitty went to the kitchen to get some water. "You were very calm after all, mother," I said.

"When I go to my dentist I usually take two aspirin tablets," she said." To visit the President, I thought I'd better take three. I guess they helped me."

"And he was so nice to you," I said. "He was genial to all of us—even after you told him I had won the election for him." "I didn't quite say that," my mother responded. "He didn't disagree with what I said. He knows you worked hard for him." "So did many other people," I reminded her. "But he was the one who won." "Oh, I know that," she said, shrugging. "I just wanted him to realize how proud I am of you. I'm sure he understood me completely."

She gazed at the book she held in her hand. "Thank God, he signed the book. Now everybody will see that we really got in to see him."

I heard a sound of knocking at the back door of the apartment. When I opened it, a red-haired boy said to me, "Terry told us you were going to the White House today to visit the President. Is that really true?" "Certainly it's true," I said. "We just got back."

I saw a long line of children behind the red-haired boy. I could feel the ripple of excitement that went through them. Apparently they had been skeptical of what Terry had told them; they suspected him of bragging. There was a moment of awed silence, and then the red-haired boy demanded, "Have you washed your hands yet?"

I was astonished. "No," I said. "Why should I?" "And you shook hands with the President?" the boy asked. "Yes," I said. "We all did. He gave Terry a pen. He'll show it to you." The boy shouted, "First of all, will you shake hands with us?" "Sure," I said. "I'll be glad to."

The children came forward one by one to shake my hand, looking deeply into my eyes to see whether I had been changed by my visit with the President in his house. They lived only a short distance from the White House, but the President was a distant figure. By taking my hand, they were getting as near to him as they could imagine.

I knew Truman's ratings in the polls were going down in that summer of 1951. There were men in the Senate who were furious at him because he had removed a hero—Douglas MacArthur. I had read letters from citizens who had urged Senators to take Truman out and hang him.

But those children wanted to get close to him. Through me, they were in touch with a man who had changed the history of the world. They knew the President's hand was full of power and might. He was the elected king of the United States.

I remembered what Truman had said about the importance of touching hands when he was running for re-election to the Senate in Missouri in 1940. He was regarded as a sure loser in that race because he had been tarred by his association with the Pendergast political organization. "I can win if I can shake enough hands," he told reporters. He went all over the state, clutching hands. And he won an upset victory—as he did in 1948.

Through me, the children touched the hand of a man who was mighty and still humble—a man who felt related to the whole human family.

In his memoirs, he declared: "I have always believed that the President's office ought to be open to as many citizens as he can find time to talk to; that is part of the job, to be available to the people, to listen to their troubles, to let them share the rich tradition of the White House...." He shared that rich tradition with my family, and I tried to share it with the children who stood in line to shake my hand that day. As I let go of the hand of the last child outside my door, I remembered how Truman had given a special gift to my son, a gift he would always cherish.

I hoped future presidents would always keep the door to the White House open for many citizens—remembering that the Executive Mansion really belonged to the people. Presidents lived there temporarily, as servants of a nation founded on the idea that governments existed to preserve the human rights of life, liberty and the pursuit of happiness.

I hoped the children who shook my hand that day would pass on to their descendants a strong belief in a constitutional society in which everyone was expected to exercise the responsibilities of free citizens in meeting the needs of all.

CHAPTER SEVENTEEN

A MAN WITH ENDURING VIRTUES—NEW GENERATIONS SEE TRUMAN'S STRENGTH

PRESIDENTS RISE AND FALL in the estimations of historians and social critics. Because the men who served in the White House in turbulent times made controversial decisions, they are always being evaluated in different terms in different periods of history. When Truman left Washington in 1953, he was surprised by the fact that many people came down to the railroad station to give him rounds of cheers. He was down again in the polls and he didn't expect the warm send-off he received.

Despite the low polls at the time, Truman has since become solidly recognized as one of the finest human beings ever to become a Chief Executive of the United States. Many of the actions he took during his years in the Oval Office will remain debatable, but even his critics do not deny the fact that Truman had fundamental virtues that were admirable and enduring.

As he went through life, he had the courage and the honesty to change his mind about many things. He overcame his prejudices, he developed friendships with a broad range of ethnic groups, he saw the necessity of bringing women into full participation in every field, he denounced fanatics who tried to fan the flames of hatred against black people and Jews, and he demonstrated his conviction that a true man's strength was best used to help the weak and the poor whenever he could.

Through all his growth and development from childhood to old age, Truman was utterly faithful to one person—Elizabeth (Bess) Wallace, with whom he fell in love when he was six years old and she was five. He saw her in the Sunday school of the Presbyterian church in Independence when she was a small girl with golden curls. He admired her then, courted her for 29 years, and finally married her. Their union

225

lasted for 53 years, and he poured out his dreams and troubles, his passionate concerns, his doubts and uncertainties, his vision of his mission in life, in the hundreds of letters he wrote to her.

Robert H. Ferrell, who edited a collection of these letters in a book entitled *Dear Bess*, describes them as "an American saga—the setting out by an astonishing letter writer the manner in which his life moved forward. The first letter shows Truman running a farm near the little Missouri village of Grandview. By the last, we hear his reflections on being president of the United States from 1945 to 1953...."

Ferrell comments; "The Truman letters show...how their author worked from morning to night trying to make the most of whatever project was at hand... It is a simply extraordinary account of what a man can do if he puts his mind and will to it... His writing shows an incessant and deep concern for other people...."

That was the key to understanding Harry Truman. His innate openness led him to realize that all human beings were connected in mysterious ways. That awareness was sparkling in his eyes, in his concentration of attention on every person who spoke to him, in his direct and warm responses to all of his staff members, to Representatives and Senators and plain citizens; in his thoughtfulness to my mother on a busy day, in his generosity to my young son and his capacity to blush when my son rejected an invitation to engage in a little mischief. He didn't react defensively when he was chided; he acknowledged his mistakes.

When he accepted the nomination for president at the Democratic convention in July 1948, after hours of tension, he stood at a podium high above the steaming floor. He was a man in a white suit, far above those who gazed at him with a mixture of doubt and hope. Yet when he began to speak I felt close to him that night—and I believe that feeling ran through all the other tired men and women in that hall.

He could have taken his nomination as a moment that certified his triumph over his opponents, that certified his greatness, his authority, his exaltation above the weary and sweltering crowd on the floor. But he didn't; his mind and his heart reached out to us. He pulled us into the joy of his victory.

With a sweeping motion of his arm, Truman said: "We are now the defenders of the stronghold of democracy and of equal opportunity, the haven of the ordinary people of this land." And we knew he meant it—he included every one of us in his vision of the future.

As I have meditated about Truman—about his impact on my life and on the lives of millions of people in several generations—I have gradually realized that he embodied the ten basic "virtues" cited in a volume entitled *The Book of Virtues* by William J. Bennett, published in 1994. Bennett was the Secretary of Education under President Ronald Reagan. His book included dozens of poems, fables, essays, speeches and stories designed to illustrate those "virtues"—ranging from self-discipline to loyalty and faith.

In western culture, we place a high value on the notion that each of us has a unique "individual self." In Truman's childhood, he was sternly admonished to master that "self" in order to reject what was "bad" and do what was "good." He was also instructed that it was necessary for him to fulfill his obligations and to carry his burdens cheerfully.

He certainly had the quality described by Bennett as "self-discipline." He did not flinch from hard tasks. He rose early and he worked hard at every job he ever had. In the presidency, he found himself compelled to do "bad things"—to order the bombings of Hiroshima and Nagasaki, to send American troops into Korea—in order to achieve "good ends:" the termination of the war with Japan, the resistance to aggression in Korea to maintain the authority of the United Nations. He suffered from severe headaches, but he accepted all the responsibilities thrust upon him.

At the front in France in 1918, some of his soldiers retreated in a panic when German explosive shells fell among them. Truman didn't run. He rallied his men and restored their confidence. He wrote to Bess about that event without being censorious: "The boys called that engagement the Battle of Who Run, because some of them ran when the first sergeant did and some of them didn't...."

The "virtue" of courage—emphasized as an important factor in every human being's life—was evident in Truman through all his years. He was brave on the battlefield in France, he was brave in facing a possible defeat when he sought re-election to the Senate in 1940, he struggled against many enemies when he gained his presidential victory in 1948, and he was brave in facing loneliness during his years in Washington, particularly when he was in the White House. His wife was frequently away and he roamed alone through the corridors of the mansion.

On one occasion he confronted what he believed to be ghosts in the old house. In a letter dated September 9, 1946, he reported to Bess: "Night before last I went to bed at nine o'clock after shutting all my doors. At four o'clock I was awakened by three distinct knocks on my bedroom door. I jumped up and put on my bathrobe, opened the door, and no one was there. Went out and looked up and down the hall, looked into your room and Margie's. Still no one. Went back to bed after locking the doors and there were footsteps in your room whose door I'd left open. Jumped and looked and no one there! The damned place is haunted, sure as shootin'... Secret Service said not even a watchman was up here at that hour... You and Margie had better come back and protect me before some of these ghosts carry me off...." He was firmly convinced that the White House was "haunted," but that conviction did not keep him from serving almost seven more years in the presidency. He faced his loneliness and his fears—and went on with his work.

William Bennett quoted statements by Truman in his book, when he discussed the importance of "perseverance." He cited Truman's remark in his *Memoirs* that being president was "like riding a tiger... A man has to keep on riding or be swallowed." Truman added that "a president is either constantly on top of events or, if he hesitates, events will soon be on top of him...." Bennett commented: "Perseverance is an essential quality of character in high-level leadership. Much good that might have been achieved in the world is lost through hesitation...."

Honesty—another quality lauded by Bennett—was also apparent in Truman's record as a public servant. Truman expressed his views so bluntly that he disturbed many people and angered others. Barry Goldwater, a very conservative Republican, expressed his admiration for Truman's integrity—and so did many other men with varying political views.

I have already noted Truman's loyalty to his friends and his principles. He was a steadfast man. He rose strongly to the defense of General George Marshall, Secretary of State Dean Acheson, and others who were vilified by Senator Joseph McCarthy. In Bennett's book, the "virtue" of loyalty is depicted in these terms: "Real loyalty endures inconvenience, withstands temptation, and does not cringe under assault." Truman did not yield to the temptation to abandon his Cabinet members and aides when they were attacked. He never cringed under any assaults.

In his discussion of the "virtue" of faith—the last fundamental "virtue" examined in his volume—Bennett wrote: "Faith contributes to the form and the content of the ideals that guide the aspirations we harbor for our own lives, and it affects the way we regard and behave with respect to others.... A human being without faith, without reverence for anything, is a human being morally adrift." Bennett referred to the results of a study made by William James, the brilliant American psychologist, who learned that people with profound spiritual convictions were almost invariably hopeful and optimistic, displaying faith in a benevolent Creator and in human beings.

Harry Truman believed the United States was the most successful nation in history because its leaders and its people generally tried to act ethically. In 1952, Truman recorded in his diary: "If I could succeed in getting the world of morals associated against the world of no morals, we'd have world peace for ages to come. Confucius, Buddha, Moses, our own Jesus Christ, Mohammed, all preached: 'Do as you'd be done by.' So did all the other great teachers and philosophers...."

In spite of all the crimes committed by human beings against one another, Truman maintained his faith in the future of humanity. In the second volume of his memoirs, he declared that what kept him going after he became president was his belief that "there is far more good than evil in men and it is the business of government to make the good prevail." He also wrote: "There is enough in the world for everyone to have plenty to live on happily and to be at peace."

Truman had his blind spots, his faults and his failings, as all men and women do. His loyalty-security program, which led to unjustified accusations against many fine persons employed by the federal government, damaged the lives of many people. But he felt that it was a necessity to have such a program during the "cold war" with the Soviet Union, and he insisted that the constitutional rights of all persons who came under investigations had to be carefully protected.

Truman felt, as I did, that the Bill of Rights was the most important part of the American Constitution. While he believed in the constructive role of government, he knew that the powers of governmental officials had to be restricted in order to preserve the essential liberties of the people. He thought that the founding leaders of the United States had shown great wisdom in devising a system of checks and balances, making it almost impossible for a dictatorship to arise.

The noted author, Thomas Merton, once said; "It is a glorious destiny to be a member of the human race." By his behavior as a man and as a public servant, Harry Truman convinced me Merton was right.

My years as a staff member of the United States Senate brought me to the edge of cynicism, but my recollections of Truman's dauntless spirit kept me from succumbing to it. After I left the Senate staff in 1952, I became involved in a series of projects—serving as the Washington director of Averell Harriman's presidential campaign in 1952, working as the U.S. director of the International Press Institute's study of world news in 1953, and helping the American Book Publishers Council beat off censorship movements in 1954.

Inspired by Truman's statement that "war—and the causes of war" must "be abolished," I became involved in the peace movement when I was elected a vice president of the Fund for the Republic, an educational organization financed by the Ford Foundation. I persuaded Robert Hutchins, president of the Fund, to convene a series of international convocations based on Pope John XXIII's encyclical letter, *Pacem in Terris* (Peace on Earth). We brought together thousands of leaders from around the world to take steps for peace. Later, I helped to create the Nuclear Age Peace Foundation, which had a vital role in a global campaign to abolish nuclear weapons.

Harry Truman saw clearly that all human beings will eventually accept the reality of being linked with everyone else on earth—and the necessity of working together as members of one family. Many of us who served under his banner in 1948 have spent our lives in efforts to build the world community he envisioned.

Truman understood the lessons of the past, and was well aware of the bloody failures of previous generations. But he was mainly a man who looked *forward*—a man who had prophetic glimpses of what humanity could achieve. He expected the triumph of the creative power which was evident to him through his experiences in the amazing days of his life.

BIBLIOGRAPHY

The following books have been consulted in the preparation of this volume:

Memoirs, Harry S. Truman. Doubleday, 1956.

Truman, David McCullough. Simon & Schuster, 1992.

Beyond the New Deal: Harry S. Truman and American Liberalism, Alonzo L. Hamby. Columbia University Press, 1973.

Harry S. Truman, Margaret Truman. William Morrow & Co 1972. (Biography by the President's daughter.)

The Truman Program: Addresses and Messages by President Harry S. Truman. Public Affairs Press, 1949.

In the Fullness of Time, Paul Douglas. Harcourt, Brace, 1972.

The Loneliest Campaign: The Truman Victory of 1948, Irwin Ross. New American Library, 1968.

Plain Speaking, Merle Miller. Berkeley, 1974.

Man of the People, Alonzo L. Hamby. Oxford, 1995.

BIOGRAPHY

CURRENTLY SENIOR VICE PRESIDENT of the Nuclear Age Peace Foundation, Frank Kelly has been active in many fields. An award-winning journalist—honored by a Nieman Fellowship at Harvard and a Wilton Park Fellowship in England—he has served as a campaign speech writer for President Truman, as a professor of communications at Boston University, as vice president of the Fund for the Republic, and as a founder of the Center for the Study of Democratic Institutions.

Following the 1948 presidential campaign, Kelly became special assistant to the Majority Leader of the U.S. Senate and held that position until 1952. He was also appointed staff director of the Majority Policy Committee. In 1952 he became the Washington director of the Harriman for President Committee. After that, he was the U.S. director of the International Press Institute's Study of World News, and then served as a consultant for the American Book Publishers Council.

In 1982, Kelly became one of the founders of the Nuclear Age Peace Foundation, which has members in many countries and is currently coordinating an international effort to abolish atomic bombs. He is an editor of the *Waging Peace Journal*, published quarterly by the Foundation. He is also a member of the board of directors of the California Center for Civic Renewal.

Frank Kelly's publications include:

An Edge of Light. Atlantic Monthly Press, 1949. A novel.
The Fight for the White House: The Story of 1912. Crowell, 1961. Story of the presidential campaign involving T. Roosevelt, Wilson, and Taft.
Your Freedoms: The Bill of Rights. Putnam's, 1964. Paper editions by Bantam and Pyramid, distributed throughout the world by U.S. Information Agency.

The Martyred Presidents and Their Successors. Putnam's, 1967.

Your Laws. Putnam's, 1970. About law making, and the roles of citizens.

Star Ship Invincible. Capra Press, 1979. Collections of science fiction stories that originally appeared in *Astounding, Amazing, and Wonder Stories* in the 1930s.

Court of Reason: Robert Hutchins & the Fund for the Republic. Macmillan/Free Press, 1981. History of the Fund and the Center for Democratic Institutions.

Kelly has contributed articles and stories to many publications, including *The Atlantic, The New Yorker,* the *Los Angeles Times,* and many newspapers. He was installed in the Science Fiction Hall of Fame in 1996, and received a Lifetime Achievement award from the *Santa Barbara News-Press* in the same year. His biography is included in the *Science Fiction Encyclopedia* and in *Who's Who in Science Fiction,* as well as in *Contemporary Authors.*